14 X 12/10 √ 3/4
20 X 1/13 √ 3/15

SHERYL LINDSELL ROBERTS

135 Tips on Email and Instant Messages

Plus Blogs, Chatrooms, and Texting

 Houghton Mifflin Company
Boston ■ New York

Visit our website: **www.houghtonmifflinbooks.com**

Library of Congress Cataloging-in-Publication Data
Lindsell-Roberts, Sheryl.
  135 tips on email and instant messages : plus blogs, chatrooms, and texting / Sheryl Lindsell-Roberts.
    p. cm.
  ISBN-13: 978-0-618-94258-9
  ISBN-10: 0-618-94258-0
  1. Electronic mail messages. 2. Business communication. I. Title.
  HD30.37.L53 2008
  651.7'9--dc22

2007048250

Manufactured in the United States of America

Book design by Catherine Hawkes, Cat & Mouse

MP 10 9 8 7 6 5 4 3 2 1

Author photograph by George Pennington; Hot tip icon photograph by Don Farrall/Photodisc Green/Getty Images; Reminder icon photograph by Stockdisc/Getty Images.

To Dawne, Marilyn, and Mark (in alphabetic order).

When I thought about dedicating this book to my in-laws, I combed the Internet to see what it had to say about in-laws. It's chock-full of jokes, horror stories, and how-to-repair-the-relationship stories. *Au contraire* when it comes to my in-laws. I feel truly blessed to have had and continue to have superb in-laws.

My parents-in-law, whom I loved and respected, meant a great deal to me and their love was a gift. I am still blessed to have Dawne, Marilyn, and Mark as part of my in-law family. They enrich my life beyond belief. I must be especially nice to Dawne and Mark because one day they'll help my children select my nursing home. And I don't want to spend my golden years in Siberia. I hate the cold!

CONTENTS

Planning Your Message 20

Crafting a Compelling Subject Line 26

Writing the Message 32

Using Proper Email Etiquette 54

E-Marketing 62

Managing Time Efficiently 74

Communicating with Teams 78

PART THREE   Text Messages, Blogs, and Chatrooms   117

"Speaking" in Chatrooms   130

ACKNOWLEDGMENTS

Special thanks . . .

to my wonderful husband, **Jon Roberts**, who sits patiently as my eyes glaze over in the middle of a conversation. It's during those times he knows I'm coming up with a dazzling idea and I'm *writing*. Shortly thereafter I'm at my computer clickety-clacking like a tenacious woodpecker. Jon helps by leaving me alone while I'm writing and by loving me alone while I'm writing.

On the professional side, I'd like to thank . . .

Marge Berube, Vice President, Publisher of Dictionaries, at Houghton Mifflin, for her continued confidence in me and for stimulating conversations when we get together for lunch.

Catherine Pratt, Editor, who is an absolute joy to work with for the third time. (I wonder if she can say the same about me.) She has lots of patience for the last-minute entries I send even as the manuscript is going to press.

Nancy Flynn, Author and Executive Director, The ePolicy Institute, who contributed survey information and quotes scattered throughout this book. The survey sponsors were the American Management Association and The ePolicy Institute.

Bard Williams, Ed.D., President and CEO, Techthree Marketing & Consulting Services, Inc., who edited Parts Two and Three for technical accuracy and provided me with on-the-spot technical guidance whenever I sent him an email with the salutation "Dear Technical Guru."

Nancy Settle-Murphy, Principal of Guided Insights (formerly Chrysalis International Corporation), who coauthored the "Communicating with Teams" section. Nancy is a facilitator of remote and face-to-face meetings. She's also a trainer, presenter, and author of many articles and white papers on getting the most out of remote teams, especially those that span cultures and time zones.

Jean Sifleet, Business Attorney, CPA, and Author, who has extensive experience in dealing with email issues in the workplace. She edited and contributed to the legal and company policy sections.

My clients, who always inspire me and who contribute immensely to my professional growth. Many of their trials and tribulations are peppered throughout this book.

INTRODUCTION

Technology . . . is a queer thing; it brings you
great gifts with one hand, and it stabs you in the
back with the other.

C. P. SNOW
English novelist and physicist

What You Don't Know C@n Hurt You!

When it comes to technology, always remember, the fire that melts butter strengthens steel. Electronic communication (emails, instant messages, text messages, blogs, and chatrooms) can be a blessing or a curse.

Email was a curse to Harry Stonecipher, Boeing CEO, who was ousted when a compromising email became public and revealed his affair with a female employee. It was a curse to Goldman Sachs when the company paid $2 million to settle federal regulators' charges for improperly offering securities through email. It was a curse to Enron when sensitive emails ended up in court as part of a congressional investigation. It was a curse to Michael Brown, head of the Federal Emergency Management Agency (FEMA), when as Hurricane Katrina savaged New Orleans he sent a message to his staff stating, "If you'll look at my lovely FEMA attire, you'll really vomit. I am a fashion god."

Instant messaging (IM) was a curse to Congressman Mark Foley when he was discovered sending inappropriate messages to teenage White House pages. And blogging was a curse to Rudy Giuliani when he was running for president of the United States and his daughter posted that she's supporting Barack Obama, Giuliani's rival in the other major political party.

Strong Communications Skills Are Critical to Your Business

On the blessing side, modern technology is responsible for . . .

- breaking down barriers. You can communicate with people in different time zones and different countries.
- accelerating teamwork. You can work remotely and keep in constant touch with the "mother ship" no matter where you are, 24/7.
- keeping you in touch with your customers. You can send instant price changes, product updates, newsletters, marketing campaigns, and more.
- having instant access to current information. You have access to the latest information on just about anything with the click of a button.

This book is for you if . . .

- email is critical to your business.
- your messages don't get you the results you want.
- you don't have the impact you want to have on your readers.
- it takes you too long to compose messages.
- you expend too much time and energy on the technology you expected to save you time and energy.
- IMing, texting, blogging, and/or chatting are creeping into your day-to-day communications.

Icons

Scattered throughout this book you'll find the following icons—somewhat like road signs—to help you find tips, reminders, and personal stories:

 Hot tip. This may be a time saver, life saver, frustration saver, or just about anything relevant to the information at hand.

 Reminder. This is a virtual string to tie around your finger so you don't forget something important, such as packing your umbrella during monsoon season.

 Word from Sheryl. This is an opportunity to share "war stories" from my experience or my clients' experiences.

A Word About Gender

Which word doesn't belong: *aunt, brother, cousin, father, grandfather, grandmother, mother, nephew, niece, sister, uncle?* The answer is *cousin* because it's the only gender-neutral term. I searched for a gender-neutral term for this book to avoid getting into the clumsy *he/she* or *him/her* pronouns but couldn't find one. So I tossed a coin, and here's how it landed: I use the male gender in the even-numbered tips and the female gender in the odd-numbered tips. (If this offends you, I apologize.)

Sheryl Lindsell-Roberts, M.A.

P.S. Keep this book for easy reference. Don't share it. You may never get it back!

PART ONE

Email

E mail—the genesis of online communication—has it all: the good, the bad, and the ugly. The good includes accelerated teamwork, boosted readerships that reach the largest possible markets, contact with virtually anyone around the globe, 24/7—and much more. The bad includes poorly written messages, some containing huge computer files that take forever to download. It also includes spams, scams, overload, junk, and ill-advised and illegal usage. The ugly includes all the unnecessary time spent reading, writing, and managing email.

These results from the 2004 *Workplace E-Mail, Instant Messaging & Blog Survey*, conducted by the American Management Association and The ePolicy Institute, show just how pervasive email has become and how much of the workday it monopolizes for both business and personal use.

Q: **On a typical workday, how much time do you spend on email?**

A:
0–59 minutes	18.5%
60–89 minutes	24.9%
90 minutes–2 hours	22.4%
2–3 hours	14.1%
3–4 hours	10.3%
4+ hours	9.9%

Q: **What percentage of the email you send/receive is personal, not business-related?**

A:
0%	14.0%
1–10%	74.4%
11–25%	8.8%
26–50%	2.0%
50+%	0.7%

Now it's your turn. Check any of the following email habits you may have. Then go to Part One to help capture the good, and get rid of the bad and the ugly.

- [ ] Sending subject lines that don't reflect the message.

- [ ] Not getting to the point at the beginning of the message.

- [ ] Responding to all (even to people who don't need to see the response).

- [ ] Not responding to messages in a timely manner.

- [ ] Sending too many attachments.

- [ ] Sending emails for issues that should be discussed on the phone or in person so you can have a two-way conversation.

- [ ] Not including proper contact information in your signature block.

- [ ] Including too many topics in one message.

- [ ] Adding people to your mailing list without getting their permission or giving them the ability to opt out.

- [ ] Using poor grammar, punctuation, and sentence structure.

Email **vs.** *E-mail* Those of you who've read my other books know that I've been spelling *e-mail* with the hyphen. Although both *e-mail* and *email* are correct and widely used, I believe the trend is to eliminate the hyphen, so I'm doing that, starting with this book. When you see *e-mail*, that's because I'm honoring a quote.

What's in an address? A lot. If you were opening a high-end advertising firm, would you want a Madison Avenue (New York) address or a Mayberry Street (Arkansas) address? The same holds true for your email address. If you're a sole proprietor or small-business owner, use your business name as part of your email address, just as larger businesses do. For example, **jackb@warnercompany.com** is a more professional address than **jackb@aol.com**. The first gives the perception of a real business; the second gives the perception of someone whose computer is sitting on the dining room table.

Using Common Sense

The difficulty . . . is not to write, but to write what you mean; not to affect your reader, but to affect him precisely as you wish.

ROBERT LOUIS STEVENSON

Email is a serious business communications tool, and you should treat it with the same respect as any other business document you write. The computer screen doesn't have the weft and feel of a sheet of paper, but that's no excuse to abandon the good habits you learned for the print medium.

Always remember that email is a legal document. (The Goldman Sachs, Boeing, Enron, Tyco, WorldCom, and Mark Foley fiascos should still be fresh in your mind.) Even if you delete an email, it can be forensically recovered and used against you in a court of law. (Check out Tips 98–103, "Understanding Legal Implications.")

1. Determine the best way to send your message.

When Raymond Tomlinson, an engineer at Bolt, Beranek & Newman, invented Internet-based email in 1971, he wanted to see if computers could exchange messages. It wasn't his intention to limit human contact, as email seems to have done.

When you need to send a message, ask yourself, What's the best way to deliver it? Email? Letter? Memo? Fax? Phone? Face to face?

I had an appointment to meet a client in downtown Boston one morning at 9:00, an appointment which I confirmed by telephone the day before. On the morning of the meeting the weather was dreadful. I knew that the heavy rain and fog would make driving slow, so I left very early. When I arrived at my client's office a little before 9:00, she looked at me quizzically and asked, "What are you doing here? Didn't you get my message?"

This is what happened: She was working late the night before, hoping to finish something in time for our meeting. She realized she wouldn't be ready, so at 8:30 in the evening she shot off an email letting me know we had to reschedule. I have a life and don't read email at 8:30 in the evening; therefore, I didn't get her message. Had she called me, I would have known not to drive in. That was clearly a situation of the sender not understanding the best means of communicating with the reader.

Following are some example scenarios and the most appropriate ways to deliver each message:

- *You want to remind Pete about a staff meeting tomorrow morning at 10:00 in Room C.*
  Email: A quick email would be appropriate.

- *It's the day of the meeting with Pete and you just found out that the meeting will be at 9:30 instead of 10:00. You must let Pete know of the change.*
  Call: You may also send an email, but make a call your first line of defense when something is time-sensitive.

- *You received a reply to an email you sent, and the person has several questions about your message.*

Call: When something is unclear to the reader, it's much more appropriate to have a two-way conversation.

- *As a high-level manager, you need to tell all employees they'll be getting paychecks twice a month, rather than every week.*
  Memo: Memos communicate a sense of importance, whereas emails communicate a sense of quickness. Even in this high-tech age, memos are a primary way for managers to communicate important information.

- *You want to send someone a warm, sincere thank-you.*
  Handwritten letter or note: A letter or note is to a passionate love affair what email is to a one-night stand.

- *You want to schedule a meeting with a client.*
  Call: It's much easier to schedule a meeting when you both have your calendars in front of you. Otherwise, there's a lot of back and forth as to who can and can't make certain dates and times.

- *You need to criticize someone's job performance.*
  Face to face: Two-way communication will give each person a chance to have her say.

- *Your colleague's father died.*
  Card or personalized note: A card offers a canned expression of sympathy, and a personalized note expresses your own special sentiment. I've read recently, however, that many people find email acceptable to express condolences because the medium offers a sense of immediacy that snail mail doesn't.

- *You want to send out a press release about your company.*
  Email followed by call: Which method of communication is more effective is an ongoing debate in the world of journalism. When you send an email, it piques inter-

est and reduces the chances of being misquoted. However, journalists may want to verify facts, ask you questions, and hear your tone of voice. To cover your bases, consider sending an email and following it up with a phone call.

- *You're part of a virtual team working under a tight deadline. All team members need to converse each morning about the progress of the project.*
  Instant messaging: This medium is quickly replacing email and the phone. You can have several screens up and several different people "talking." The session can be saved and used to track the project.

Commend through email. The reader is apt to print out your message, read it many times, and show it to others. This magnifies the event. *Chastise verbally.* Although no one likes to be chastised, a conversation fades with time. If you chastise someone via email, the recipient may read the message many times, and dwell on your words.

2. Understand how people read.

Before you can write any email, you must understand how people read. They don't read emails as they read *War and Peace*. They don't put their feet up on the table in front of a roaring fire and immerse themselves in every pearly word. Don't ever expect readers to examine your email prose from start to finish. People do a quick scan, which is an initial inspection of the headlines and anything else that pops out. If you've captured their attention, they'll usually read the opening paragraph and take a look at the bullets. They'll also glance at charts and tables. If they like what they see, they may read the entire document.

With email, as opposed to hard copy, you have a more difficult task. If your message spans more than one screen, people must page down to do even a quick scan. So, you must capture their attention first in the subject line, then in the opening paragraph. This is even more critical when people read email on hand-held computers because they have a very limited viewing area. (Check out Tips 24 and 28.)

3. Don't glut cyberspace with digital dross.

Your company's email isn't the place to announce you're having your annual garage sale or you're selling cookies for your daughter's Girl Scout troop. See if your company has allotted space on their intranet, blog, or electronic bulletin board for non-work-related announcements.

And be wary of what you receive. Companies aren't offering free trips to Bora Bora, there's no organ donor theft ring in Kalamazoo, and Colonel Sanders isn't selling his chicken recipes. Even if a rocket crashed and plutonium was spreading over the entire Northern Hemisphere, do you really think such information would be sent via email?

4. Never assume your intended reader received (or read) your message.

There are all sorts of reasons the intended reader may not have received or seen your email. Here are just a few:

- **You inadvertently sent the message to the wrong address.** My colleague's name is Jan Richards, and her email address is **jrichards@company.com**. Someone in her office is named Jack Richardson, and his email address is **jrichardson@company.com**. As you can well imagine, they invariably get each other's emails.

- **You were spammed out.** Your email may have landed in the recipient's spam box.

- **The recipient missed it.** People are so bombarded with emails, they may not read them all.

- **The message never arrived.** As strange as this seems, not all emails reach their destinations.

If you don't hear back from someone in a reasonable time, assume he didn't see your message. Either send another email or pick up the phone. If you need to confirm that your reader received your message, use the Request Read Receipt option. (Check out Tip 50.)

> Three months after my dear friend died, I received an email from her asking me to meet her for lunch. My breathing quickened. My heart pounded. My palms sweated. After I regained my composure, I looked at the date. She had sent the message six months *before* she died. That email was floating around in the vast digital wilderness of cyberspace for nine months.

5. Write reader-focused messages.

Everything you write should be about your reader, not about you. The harsh reality is your reader probably doesn't care about you. Advertisers know the importance of using a tone that "talks" directly to the reader. Notice how often the words *you* and *your* appear in the headlines of advertisements.

Be careful, however, that you don't insult the reader with the *you* approach. It would be in good taste to write, "We're sorry for the delay. We'll have our shipping department look into it and accept responsibility if we're at fault." It would be in poor taste to write, "Your error caused the delay, and you will see extra charges on your next invoice."

6. Respect international and cultural differences.

Email cuts across world cultures and spans all time zones. Be mindful of the following when sending email to people of other cultures:

Formality	People in many countries find the friendly nature of Americans overbearing at first. Always address people by their last names until you establish a first-name relationship.
Tone	• Create a friendly yet businesslike tone. • Minimize abbreviations and acronyms. If you must use them, explain them. • Avoid slang and jargon. • Use simple vocabulary and conventional syntax. • Over-explain, rather than under-explain.
Communication styles	Understand the difference in cultural forces. For example, people in the US are known for taking quick action and "cutting to the chase." Our counter-

parts in Japan prefer pre-planning and deliberating to build consensus. Also, be aware of regional differences within the same country.

Sarcasm and humor   Avoid sarcasm and humor in all business situations, but especially when you're communicating with people of different cultures. Many points have been missed and international contacts lost due to the misunderstanding of humor.

Time differences   Always answer emails as soon as you can. But remember that your email may arrive during your recipient's off-work hours or on a holiday you don't know about. So, be patient before resending the same message or sending a follow-up message.

Dates   When sending an international email that includes dates, be sure to use the appropriate conventions. For example, in European countries and in the military, the day comes before the month (for example, 2 March 2008), and March 2 would be abbreviated 2/3. When possible, avoid abbreviating dates so you don't create confusion.

Time of day   Be aware that most countries use the 24-hour clock. For example, 3:30 PM would be written as 15:30.

Contact information   Always provide proper international dialing telephone codes and contact

	information when sending emails over-seas.
Monetary translations	When mentioning currency, use either the currency of both countries or the currency of the country in which the financial dealings take place.
Measurements	Most countries use the metric system. You may be wise to show the American and metric equivalents, for example, "1 inch (25 millimeters)."

7. Don't be scammed by phishers or pharmers.

Institutions such as banks, credit card companies, eBay, PayPal, Internet service providers (ISPs), the government, and others will never ask for personal information such as your credit card number, PIN, social security number, date of birth, mother's maiden name, and more via email. If you get a legitimate-looking email from such an institution requesting this type of information, you've been scammed. Do not open these emails, and never give out any information. There are two terms for these types of scams:

- *phishing* (pronounced *fishing*), in which users receive a fraudulent email that looks authentic and appears to be sent from someone they do business with.

- *pharming* (pronounced *farming*), in which users are unknowingly directed to a bogus website through technical means.

To avoid being the "catch of the day," establish a free account (such as on Yahoo or Hotmail), and don't use your real name. Use this account to make online purchases and inquiries.

Scamming is different from *spamming*. Spams are emails sent without your consent, generally to promote a service or product. By the way, Spam (short for "spiced ham") is a luncheon meat made by Hormel Foods. The word *spam* became popular slang following a Monty Python skit.

8. Send attachments only if you're sure your reader can receive and read them.

Many organizations and industries use software the average person typically doesn't have. (For example, architects may use Archi-CAD and accountants may use Peachtree.) If readers don't have that software installed on their machines, they won't be able to receive the files. Check before you send. Also, check to see that your reader can receive a very large file.

Attachments can carry viruses, take time to download, and take up space on the reader's computer. If the attachment isn't long and doesn't have lots of formatting, cut and paste the message into the text. Following are a few suggestions for when you must send attachments:

- **Let the reader know what file format you're sending.** Even with the same software vendor, files aren't necessarily *downwardly compatible* (able to be read by a previous version of the software).

- **If an attached file is long, compress it.** Files compressed in programs such as WinZip can speed delivery and cut down on network traffic. Let the reader know what program you used to compress the document so he can uncompress the file on his end.

- **Use a free service.** When you need to send large files, consider sending them through **www.sendthisfile.com**. This is a free service and there's no file size limit.

 Different rules for PDAs Always remember that your reader may be viewing your message on a PDA. If you send an attachment, summarize the essence of the attachment in a brief opening paragraph. If you cut and paste from another format (such as an Excel spreadsheet), be aware that the PDA may not display the information pasted. Instead of seeing the information, the reader may see the word *Insert*.

How many times have you gotten an email and the sender forgot to append the attachment mentioned? If you tend to forget to append attachments (and who doesn't?), append the attachment *before* you fill in the *To:* field. Also, it's a good idea to open the attachment to make sure you attached the correct one.

Responding to online job postings I'm often asked, "When you respond to a job posting online, do you include the cover letter in the body of the message?" People don't like to open too many attachments, so here are two alternatives:

- Send your cover letter and professional-looking resume as a single-file attachment. Include the cover letter as the first page and the resume as the second.

- If you don't want to send an attachment, create a brief summary of your resume, followed by your complete resume, and paste it into the text box.

Regardless of which option you choose, send the letter and resume by regular US mail if the company address is available.

This will help you to cover your bases. Mention in the email that you're sending hard copy also.

9. Forward selectively.

Forwarding messages is a wonderful way to pass legitimate business-related information to others who need the information. Here are some tips:

- Decide if you should change the subject line so it represents your message to your readers.

- Consider how much of the message you need to send, and forward only what your reader needs to see.

- Eliminate the dross of mail headers and other detritus email picks up on the forwarding circuit. That includes the > symbol letting the reader know the message has been around the world a gazillion times.

10. Manage your email when you're away for extended periods of time.

When you're away from the office, whether on a romantic getaway or an extended business trip, manage your messages. Here are a few suggestions for curtailing the tsunami of email:

- Create an out-of-office, auto-reply message. You can create an auto-reply to all your inbound messages letting senders know you're away. You can also have your messages stored on the server or forwarded to another e-address. Remember to turn off the auto-reply when you return. A word of caution: When you initiate auto-reply, you're notifying spammers of a valid address.

- Take yourself off noncritical distribution lists. You can do this by unsubscribing, then resubscribing when you return.

11. Use terminology appropriate for your reader.

Always be sure your reader will understand your terminology. Technical jargon, when used properly, can be a hallmark of good writing to readers with knowledge in the subject area. In these cases, it makes no sense to water down the language; doing so may damage the integrity of your message and insult the reader. When you write to people outside your industry, avoid technical terms. Use plain language your reader will understand.

12. Think seriously about being funny.

Humor is sensitive. Will Rogers once said, "Everything is funny as long as it is happening to somebody else." If there's the slightest chance your humor may be mistaken for sarcasm, avoid it. And if you do intend to be sarcastic, think carefully before you commit your scorn to the written word; it may come back to haunt you. Even among friends, humor can be cutting.

George Bernard Shaw once sent tickets for his latest play to his good friend Winston Churchill. Mr. Shaw included this note: "Here are two tickets to my new play. Bring a friend—if you have one." Mr. Churchill returned the tickets with this note: "Sorry, I'm unable to attend opening night. Please send me tickets for the second performance—if there is one."

 Used effectively, humor can get and hold the reader's attention. Check out this example:

Half the battle in communicating effectively by e-mail is getting the other party just to open your message. In a spam-filled world, the ability to craft a compelling subject line is an art—not a science. That is why we were particularly impressed by a catchy missive sent our direction by EMC spokesman Michael Gallant, who wrote, "Are you drinkin' the Bloomin' Kool-Aid"?

—Mark Veverka, "EMC and Veritas Swap Insults Over Storage Efforts," *Barron's*

"Drinking the Kool-Aid" is a term used in the public relations field that dates back to the Jonestown massacre of 1978—a mass suicide in which the followers of cult leader Jim Jones drank a mixture of Kool-Aid, cyanide, and tranquilizers. Gary Bloom was a high-ranking executive at one of EMC's competitors. This was a very captivating subject line with humor that did the job!

13. Proofread until your eyeballs hurt.

People often feel that it's okay to send email messages with errors. That is absolutely untrue. *Email is a serious business communications tool and you should treat it with the same respect as any other business document you write.* You often send emails to people you've never met, and they form an impression of you based on your message. What do you want that impression to be? (Check out Tips 42–49, "Proofreading and Editing.")

Don't be like my colleague, the public relations director, who sent an email to more than a thousand colleagues in the United States, Europe, and Asia. She left the *l* out of *Public* in the signature portion. Think about that for a moment! (Check out Tip 56.)

Planning Your Message

It wasn't raining when Noah built the ark.

HOWARD RUFF
American business consultant

In order to write a clear and concise message—one that's reader-focused—you must understand who your readers are, what they need to know, the one key point they should remember, and the questions they'll want answered. This section will walk you through the planning process.

14. Get into your reader's head.

Why is it so easy to send an email to a friend or colleague you know well? Obviously, because you know him. You know his preconceived ideas, his level of experience, and probably his reaction to your message. You must try to know any reader. If the message is to someone you don't know, try to imagine what he looks like. In that way you're not writing to a faceless humanoid.

Identify your reader and the relationship (if any) that you have with him. Is he a manager, peer, subordinate, customer, client, salesperson, decision maker? Remember that you must see your target so you know where to aim.

15. Determine if you have multiple levels of readers.

When you write to multiple readers, rank them on the basis of who will take action or in their order of importance. If you're writing to a mixed audience of managers, technical people, and salespeople, consider dealing with each audience in separate emails.

16. Ask yourself what your reader needs to know about the topic.

Needs to know are the key words. You don't want to give your reader too much or too little information. Ask yourself these questions:

- What's the reader's level of knowledge about the subject?
- Does he have any preconceived notions?
- Are there barriers to his understanding the message?

17. Anticipate what's in it for your reader.

When you receive a message, you undoubtedly ask yourself, Why is this worth my time? Your reader will ask the same question. Understand why this message is worth your reader's time. Perhaps this is a chance to make her job easier, help her look good to her superiors, acquire more knowledge, or make more money. Make it clear what's in it for her!

My newspaper carrier nailed this concept. He put an envelope in my newspaper (for me to enclose a tip) and included this note: "Throughout the winter months, I'm glad I was able to deliver your newspaper to your doorstep every day, on time." Do you think I gave him a larger-than-normal tip? You bet I did.

18. Ask yourself what your reader's attitude will be when he receives your message.

You may not always tell your reader what he wants to hear, but you must tell him what he *needs* to hear. When you anticipate your reader's reaction, you can sequence the message for greater impact. (Check out Tip 30.) Following are the three reactions your reader may have:

Reaction	What it means	Example
Responsive	Your reader will be happy to get your message.	You're sending your reader information he requested.
Neutral	Your reader won't feel strongly one way or the other.	You're informing your reader that his subscription or membership is about to expire.
Unresponsive	Your reader won't be happy to get your message.	Your message will mean more work for your reader.

19. Identify the action item.

When your reader knows exactly what action you want her to take, she can digest your message more intelligently and respond accordingly. Use headlines to call out the action item. (Check out Tip 29.) Do you want the reader to . . .

- call you?
- send a check?
- discontinue testing?
- send you information?
- do nothing?

20. Distill the one key point you want your reader to remember.

Billboard advertisers, ad people, and designers know that reading is done on the fly. Kids know this too. Have you ever found (or left) a note on the table saying "Please leave me $5—I'll explain later"? Business readers want the key issue so they can get to the point immediately. Put on your advertising hat.

If your reader forgets just about everything in your message, what's the one key point you want him to remember? (This refrain should be like an "earworm," a song that keeps repeating in your head.) It's only after you distill the message into a single sentence that you're ready to write your email.

 If the message is delivering good or neutral news, consider making the key point your subject line.

21. Ask yourself the questions your reader will ask.

Newspaper reporters use the *who, what, when, where, why,* and *how* technique to guide readers through stories. You can use the same approach so your reader doesn't have to email back or call asking for information you forgot to include. For example, if I'm inviting you to a meeting, you will probably have the following questions:

Who will be there?
What is the agenda?
When is the meeting?
Where will the meeting be held?
(*Why* has already been answered by *what.*)
How can I prepare?

22. Answer the questions.

Your answers should be specific, not vague. For example, if the meeting will be held in Washington, specify Washington, DC, or the state of Washington. Following are examples of answers to the questions in Tip 21. (Check out Tip 29 to see how the message might read.)

Who will be there? Christine, Dean, Anthony, Alyssa, and Amanda.
What is the agenda? Plans to launch our new website.
When is the meeting? June 15, 20—, at noon.
Where will the meeting be held? Conference Room 405.
Why are we meeting? (*What* answered this.)
How can I prepare? Bring the outlines you've been working on.

Never use *as soon as possible* or *ASAP*. They aren't precise. When you need something by a certain date, give the date.

23. Compose headlines that address the answers to the questions.

As mentioned in Tip 2, people do a quick scan, which is an initial check of the headlines. This is why newspapers are such a quick way to gather information. You can read a newspaper headline and get a key piece of information without reading the article.

The Broadway producer Hal Prince was asked how he could predict if a show would be a success or a flop once it had opened. Prince responded that the day after a show debuts, he opens the newspaper—the headlines dictate the fate of his show. Headlines are powerful, and you can apply that same power to your emails. Use headlines to . . .

- give directions
- offer results
- make recommendations
- get a response.

Here are some headlines to consider using:

Action Requested
Next Step
Results
Recommendations
Deadline: [date]

Crafting a Compelling Subject Line

Treat subject lines like newspaper headlines.

MICHAEL GOLDBERG
quoting Sheryl Lindsell-Roberts,
CIO magazine, June 1, 2003

The subject line is the most important piece of information in an email. It stands alone to pull in your audience without the benefit of context. Your words are trapped inside a field with competing subject lines, unable to set themselves apart. If your subject line doesn't seduce the reader, he may never open your message.

Compelling subject line leads to major recognition for a nationally known technology company The manager of public relations and leading spokesperson for a nationally known technology company attended my business writing workshop, which covers email savvy. At the end of the day, a major competitor made an announcement that would have an incredible impact on the industry. Without contacting the PR manager's company for comment, a news wire service quickly issued a story.

Because this story was to be carried by major newspapers the next day, it was imperative for the PR manager to get his company's message to the editor of the wire service very quickly and very clearly in the hope that the editor would issue an update. He told me he sat at his computer and asked himself, How would Sheryl handle this? Remembering what he had just learned at the workshop, he …

- wrote a compelling subject line that instantly captured the attention of the editor.

- started the message with solid "sound bites" containing the key information that he wanted to appear in his company's version of the story.

- supported the key information with background facts and comments.

By composing a compelling subject line and strategic message, the PR manager got control of a story that would be read by hundreds of thousands of readers. His company's version of the story was printed in the leading newspapers via the wire service, giving the company instant credibility and educating readers as to how this company is superior to its competitors. The relationship between the PR manager and the news wire service has continued to flourish, and the company is now recognized as the industry leader in its technology space. *The power of a clear, concise, and well-written subject line and message is immeasurable.*

24. Write a meaningful subject line.

There are people who get hundreds of email messages a day, and they can't possibly read them all. Your subject line must compel the reader to open your message. If you look down the subject line column of your inbox, perhaps you see subject lines such as these that give you absolutely no information and no reason to read the message:

Billing
Two things . . .
Thanks
About Jim
Update

Now compare those to a newspaper headline. When you look down the left column in each section of most major newspapers, you can read the headlines and get a snapshot of significant stories. Wouldn't it be helpful if you could read the subject column of your inbox and get that same level of information? You can.

Sending a message the reader will view as positive or neutral

Always include in your subject line a key piece of information so your reader can get the gist of your message at a glance. Notice the following pairs of subject lines and how much more compelling the second one (→) is.

Profit report → 15% profit expected for Q2
Sales meeting → Rescheduling 5/5 sales mtg to 5/6 at 2:30
Contact you requested → Contact Jane Brown at Mellows Co.
June 5 → Deadline moved to June 5
Possible dates → Would July 6, 7, or 8 work?
New hire → Brad Jones joining Mktg. Grp. April 5
About Mark → Mark Jones still interested, but not ready
　　　　　　　to sign

A potential client had been sending me emails with the subject line "I need to talk to you." I didn't recognize the name, and the subject line didn't distinguish itself from the deluge of spam I get each day. So, I kept deleting the message. The sender finally called the person who referred her, and we straightened things out. This was a classic case of a poorly written subject line and the wrong form of communication.

When I didn't respond, the sender should have picked up the phone, rather than assume I was ignoring her. A clear subject line would have been "I was referred by Steve Greir." That would have caught my attention, and I would have responded immediately.

Sending a message the reader will view as negative

When you send negative news, use a neutral subject line. For example, if the profit is expected to decrease in Q2, use a subject line such as "Q2 Profit Report." In this way you have a chance to sequence the message so you don't hit the reader between the eyes with negative news. (Check out Tip 30.)

 When you abbreviate, be certain the reader will understand your abbreviations. For example, in the United States, we recognize 5/6 as May 6. In Europe or in the military, they recognize 5/6 as June 5. And the ABA can be the American Bar Association, the American Banking Association, the American Booksellers Association, the American Basketball Association, or the anything-with-a-B association.

25. Use key words in the subject line.

Using a key word (or key words) at the start of your subject line can be helpful when forwarding a message to someone else or trying to locate an old message on a topic. Some key words may be *MIS, Billing, Human Resources (HR), Meeting, New Products, Website, March launch,* or anything else that will serve as a trigger.

 Remember that the average subject line displays about 35 characters.

26. Determine if you can deliver your message in the subject line.

When the message itself can fit into the subject line, let the subject line deliver your message. End with a sign-off such as your name, your initials, *END*, or *EOM* (for *end of message*), and you won't need to write anything in the text box. Here's an example:

> I'll finish the Marric report tomorrow morning /Pat

Avoid using this type of electronic shorthand when you write to someone you don't know. It's for colleagues with whom you communicate regularly. However, you should always use a descriptive subject line:

> I'll finish the Marric report tomorrow morning

27. Change the subject line when replying.

When you reply to someone's message, change the subject line. To maintain continuity in a stream of messages, use the key word in the subject line and add the change to the message. Here's an example:

> Billing: To be discussed at April mtg.

My colleague, James, tells the story of coming to work one foggy morning and noticing that someone left the car lights on. He sent an email to the entire distribution list with the subject line "Lic. #234 ADB car lights on." Realizing that James was in the office, people took the opportunity to send him their own messages. One person asked James to meet her for lunch; another wanted to find out when a seminar was being offered; and another wanted some other information. None of the people changed the subject line from "Lic. #234 ADB car lights on," although none of the messages had anything to do with the one James sent.

Writing the Message

*You don't write because you want to
say something; you write because you
have something to say.*

F. SCOTT FITZGERALD
The Crack-Up

You may have heard the story of the aspiring novelist who
kept rewriting the opening sentence. He never got beyond the
first sentence because he didn't have a structure. The sections
"Planning Your Message" and "Crafting a Compelling Subject
Line" gave you structure. Now you're ready to write your
message.

28. Apply the questioning technique to compose the first paragraph.

Once you capture the reader's attention, he'll probably read the
first paragraph. (Check out Tip 21 to be sure you give your
reader all the key information at a glance.) Being concise is
especially helpful to people who will read your message on a
PDA, which has a very small viewing screen.

 There are times it's wise to include the action item first.
For example, "Please reserve your space for the [whatever] by [date] because seating is limited."

29. Write headlines that give critical information.

You can apply the power of newspaper headlines to all your emails. As a writer, you direct your reader's attention to what's important. As a reader, you get the gist of the message and find key information quickly. Here's how you can apply headlines to an email inviting people to the meeting mentioned in Tip 22.

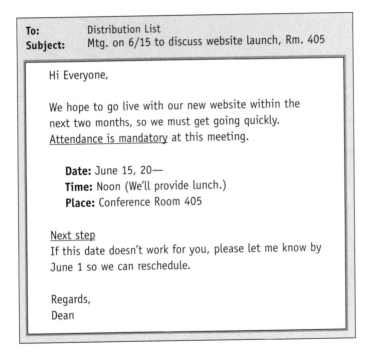

> **To:** Distribution List
> **Subject:** Mtg. on 6/15 to discuss website launch, Rm. 405
>
> ---
>
> Hi Everyone,
>
> We hope to go live with our new website within the next two months, so we must get going quickly. <u>Attendance is mandatory</u> at this meeting.
>
> **Date:** June 15, 20—
> **Time:** Noon (We'll provide lunch.)
> **Place:** Conference Room 405
>
> <u>Next step</u>
> If this date doesn't work for you, please let me know by June 1 so we can reschedule.
>
> Regards,
> Dean

30. Sequence your message for maximum impact.

In Tip 18 we discussed anticipating the reaction of your reader (responsive, neutral, or unresponsive). You have a strong impact on your reader when you sequence the message properly, even if you deliver bad news.

Putting good news or neutral news up front

When you send a message your reader will view as good or neutral news, put the key message at the beginning. (After all, this isn't a joke where you have to put the punch line at the end.) This type of message is easy to write because everyone likes to be the bearer of good news. Consider delivering the key issue in the subject line:

> Yes, we can meet your deadline of 12/5/XX.
> We accept your offer!

Cushioning news for an unresponsive reader

There are times you must say no or deliver information the reader won't want to hear. When you must disappoint the reader, you need special planning. Following are suggestions for delivering a message to an unresponsive reader:

- Open with a buffer, explain the decision, and close on a friendly note.

- Offer options, if you can. For example, if a student is applying to a university for funding and he isn't eligible for that funding, point him in the direction of other funding options.

- Give a reason. People accept what they understand.

- Accentuate the positive.

The following are two examples of a message delivering bad news from a company that needed to tell employees they'll be issuing paychecks every two weeks rather than every week. They expected a lot of grumbling.

After: Giving a reason and accentuating the positive

> With operating costs rising, we have been looking for
> ways to cut costs without cutting jobs or benefits.
> Rather than cutting staff, rather than asking employees
> to contribute more to their health insurance premiums,
> and rather than cutting our 401K match, we have found
> a way to keep all your jobs and benefits intact.
>
> We will be issuing paychecks every two weeks, rather
> than every week, starting on [date]. If you feel this will
> create a cash-flow problem, we are offering free budget-
> ing assistance through the EAP on the following dates:

Before: Jumping in with the bad news

> To save money, we find it necessary to issue paychecks
> every two weeks rather than every week. We hope this
> won't be a problem for you. If it is, we are offering free
> budgeting assistance through the EAP on the following
> dates:

31. Use proper capitalization and punctuation.

Unless you're e. e. cummings, use proper capitalization so readers can decode your sentences. All lowercase makes your message
difficult to read because your reader isn't getting visual clues.

> dear tom, let's see if we can meet tomorrow after work.
> does that work for you? bob

All uppercase makes your reader think you're screaming. It is also difficult to read.

> DEAR TOM, LET'S SEE IF WE CAN MEET TOMORROW AFTER WORK. DOES THAT WORK FOR YOU? BOB

Use proper punctuation so your reader can decode your sentences. Place punctuation marks in the message below to see what you get:

No proper capitalization and no punctuation

> DEAR PAT I WANT A MAN WHO KNOWS WHAT LOVE IS ALL ABOUT YOU ARE GENEROUS KIND THOUGHTFUL PEOPLE WHO ARE NOT LIKE YOU ADMIT TO BEING USELESS AND INFERIOR YOU HAVE RUINED ME FOR OTHER MEN I YEARN FOR YOU I HAVE NO FEELINGS WHATSOEVER WHEN WE'RE APART I CAN BE HAPPY FOREVER WILL YOU LET ME BE YOURS CHRIS

Here are two possible ways to decode this message:

A warm and caring message

> Dear Pat,
>
> I want a man who knows what love is all about. You are generous, kind, thoughtful. People who are not like you admit to being useless and inferior. You have ruined me for other men. I yearn for you. I have no feelings whatsoever when we're apart. I can be happy forever. Will you let me be yours?
>
> Chris

A cold and distant message

> Dear Pat,
>
> I want a man who knows what love is. All about you
> are generous, kind, thoughtful people who are not like
> you. Admit to being useless and inferior. You have
> ruined me. For other men I yearn. For you I have no
> feelings whatsoever. When we're apart I can be happy
> forever. Will you let me be?
>
> Yours,
> Chris

Lost in the e-translation When you write a message,
be aware that the recipient may not *see* what you wrote.
This is especially true for people who read email on hand-held
computers. For example, tabs and bullets don't always survive
the trip through cyberspace. Here are a few suggestions:

- Instead of using bullets, use asterisks (*), greater-than
  symbols (>), hyphens (-), or other keyboard characters.

- Use the space bar, rather than the tab key.

- When you use boldface, add some other way to emphasize
  the text. You may write *** **Deadline: May 5** ***. Even
  if the bold doesn't appear, the reader will still see
  *** Deadline: May 5 ***, which will be prominent.

Fine-Tuning the Message

Our life is frittered away by detail....
Simplify, simplify.

HENRY DAVID THOREAU
Walden

You don't need a degree in graphics to put together a good-looking email that will have the impact you want. This section offers many hints.

32. Use white space appropriately.

White space is all the area on the screen where there's no type. People take for granted that white space is something they should have, but they don't always know why or how to create it. Following are a few ways to use white space for a strong visual impact:

- Keep paragraphs to about eight lines of text.

- Leave a line space between each paragraph.

- Create a line space above and below a bulleted or numbered list.

- Emphasize key pieces of text. For example, if you want

to call out the date, time, and place of a meeting, consider this format:

Date: March 20
Time: 1:00–3:30
Place: Conference Room 2

33. Use an easy-to-read font, such as Ariel 10.

Ariel 10 is the recommended font choice for email, and many email software programs default to it. Ariel, a sans serif typeface, is crisp and easy to read on a computer screen. It doesn't have any of the doodads of a serif font. Notice the difference:

Times Roman is a standard serif font.
Ariel is a standard sans serif font.

Perhaps you want to personalize your emails to suit your taste and use a Chiller font. If your business is selling fright wigs, you can probably get away with that. Otherwise, be more conventional; you want to be taken seriously. Wichita State University recently studied how your choice of fonts is perceived by your reader. Senders were seen as stable/unstable, exciting/dull, formal/casual, assertive/passive, creative/unimaginative, and more—all based on their font choice.

34. Create bulleted and numbered lists, when appropriate.

Use bulleted lists when rank or sequence aren't important. Bullets give everything on the list equal value.

You can use his advice in the following situations:

- selecting a vendor
- agreeing on a price
- issuing the order
- paying the invoice.

Use numbered lists when items are listed in order or are steps in a sequence. Numbers indicate priority.

You can use his advice in the following situations:

1. selecting a vendor
2. agreeing on a price
3. issuing the order
4. paying the invoice.

35. Eliminate anything that doesn't add value.

The less you say the more impact you'll have on your reader, so skip the picayune details. Try to imagine that every word you use will cost you $100. Perhaps that will motivate you to cut to the bare essentials. Eliminate any word, phrase, sentence, or paragraph that doesn't add value. It's interesting to note that the Gettysburg Address—probably one of the most notable speeches ever—was only 278 words.

Following are examples of phrases to avoid and what can replace them.

make reference to → refer to
come to an agreement → agree
extend an invitation → invite, ask
give an indication of → indicate, show

Studies show that women have different email communication styles from men, causing them to be taken less seriously. Women tend to . . .

- be more chatty before getting to the point.
- look for validation with questions such as, "Don't you agree?"
- use "I" references more often.

An interesting book about gender differences in communications is *Gender and Communication at Work*, edited by Mary Barrett and Marilyn J. Davidson.

36. Limit sentences to 25 words or less.

Keep it short and simple. The articles of World War II correspondent Ernie Pyle, the columns of Ann Landers, and the speeches of Sir Winston Churchill all share something in common—an average sentence length of 15 words.

37. Use positive words and thoughts.

Using positive words and thoughts engages the reader's goodwill and enhances your tone. Sometimes it's merely a matter of saying what you can and will do, rather than what you can't or won't do.

Positive: We hope you'll be delighted with the test results.

Negative: We hope you won't be disappointed with the test results.

Positive: We can charge orders of $20 or more.
Negative: We can't charge orders under $20.

 I was writing a user manual for one of my clients who invented an electrical appliance. On the cover he asked me to put "This is no more dangerous than a hair dryer." The word *dangerous* would have stood out like a neon sign, so I wrote, "This is as safe as a hair dryer."

When you use the negative, do so because there's a reason to.

38. Create "sound" with punctuation.

When you speak aloud, you constantly punctuate with your voice and body language. When you write, you also make a sound in the reader's head. You do it with punctuation. It can be a dull mumble, a joyful expression, a neutral sound, or a shy whisper. It depends on the punctuation you use. Notice how em dashes, parentheses, and commas can be used interchangeably for a different emphasis:

- **Em dashes** around parenthetical text—instead of commas—strongly call out what's enclosed in the dashes. (You can represent an em dash by typing two hyphens.)

- **Parentheses** around parenthetical text (instead of em dashes or commas) downplay what's enclosed in the parentheses.

- **Commas** around parenthetical text, rather than em dashes or parentheses, neutralize what's enclosed in the commas.

- **Question marks** automatically signal interactivity, because they get the reader involved. When the question is thought-provoking, it makes a good opener that compels the reader to think a certain way.

- **Exclamation points** create excitement. (Two exclamation points, however, are weak, because they betray the sense of excitement.)

- **Colons** push the reader into what follows, propelling the concept of the incompleteness of what's been said before.

39. Be thoughtful when using industry-specific jargon.

Whether to use jargon depends on knowing your reader and your reader's level of industry knowledge. If your reader is outside your industry, refrain from using jargon. If your reader is part of your industry, use your jargon. Watering down the language may damage the integrity of the email and insult your reader.

I was on a flight waiting to take off when the pilot announced that the takeoff would be delayed because of a slight problem in the "aft lav on the port." As a sailor, I understood his jargon, but people around me had to ask the flight attendant for a translation. (*Aft* means "rear" and *port* means "left." *Lav* referred to the lavatory.) Please speak plain language, Mr. Pilot.

40. Never replace technical terms with synonyms.

Repeating a word is better than compromising the integrity of what you write. For example, if you change *computer networks* to *computer systems*, you alter the meaning.

41. Be consistent with your wording.

If you make reference to a *user manual*, don't later call it a *reference manual, guide,* or *document.* Your readers won't know whether you're referring to the same publication or different ones.

 Avoid the words *yesterday, today,* and *tomorrow.* They're relative to when the reader views your message, rather than when you send the message. Give the date instead.

Proofreading and Editing

*How would you like a job where, if you
made a mistake, a big red light goes on and
18,000 people boo?*

JACQUES PLANTE
former National Hockey League goalie

What would you do if you went to a fine restaurant and the menu included items such as *white whine, soap of the day, baked zits,* and *turkey coffee*? You'd probably run out as fast as you could. You don't want your readers to run visually. Proofread and edit carefully. Notice the difference in the following sentences when you change the position of the colon:

Execution: impossible to be pardoned.
Execution impossible: to be pardoned.

Don't turn on your computer and turn off your brain. The computer is a wonderful tool for checking spelling and grammar, but it's just that—a tool. Check, double-check, and triple-check spelling, grammar, and punctuation yourself. There's nothing like the human eye.

A client sent me what was supposed to be a glowing testimonial for my business writing workshop. She wrote, "One person remarked that a document that used to take him four hours to write is now taking him two years [instead of two hours]." When I brought this to her attention, we had a good laugh and she made the correction.

42. Check the accuracy of all names, including middle initials, and titles.

Many people are incensed when you misspell their names. Always double-check the spelling. For example, do you spell the recipient's name *Carroll, Carol,* or *Carole*? Additionally, don't assume you know the sex of a person by the name. Carroll O'Connor is a man, and Stevie Nicks is a woman. Pat, Chris, and many other names are gender-neutral.

If you're unsure of the spelling, check your file or the Internet, or call the person directly and say, "I'm going to be sending you [whatever] and want to make sure I spell your name correctly. Would you please spell it for me."

> If you don't know the gender of the reader, and you don't know the person well enough to call him by his first name, use the person's full name in the salutation, for example, "Hi, Chris Mason . . ."

43. Confirm company designations.

Make sure you use *Company, Co., Inc., Incorporated, Limited, Ltd.,* or whatever the company uses. And spell the company name correctly. I know of a situation where Emory University issued an RFP (request for proposal) for a very large project. On the cover of one of the proposals, a submitter wrote "Emery." That proposal went in the trash—unread.

44. Double-check all numbers.

It's easy to omit a number or transpose numbers and not realize it. This can cause serious problems. One of my clients placed an ad in a major publication and inadvertently transposed the last two digits of the phone number. When people called, they reached a sex hotline. Oops!

45. Keep an eye out for misused or misspelled homophones.

Homophones are words that sound the same but are spelled differently. You need to know the difference because your computer doesn't. Here are two troublesome pairs and how to distinguish them.

Principal and *principle*: *Principal* means "main" or "sum of money." *Principle* means "rule" or "value."

The strike is the *principal* reason for the delay.
Please apply $200 to the *principal* owed on my loan.
Freedom of speech is a *principle* of democracy.
He is a man of high *principles*.

Stationery and *stationary*: *Stationery* means "paper" (note the *-er* ending). *Stationary* means "immovable."

The *stationery* aisle is the third one on your left.
The cabinets are *stationary*; it would take a crane to move them.

46. Be on the alert for small words that you repeat or misspell.

It's easy to write *it* instead of *is* and not realize it. Your computer won't know the difference, but your reader will. Also, be on the lookout for other misspellings your computer won't detect. For example, an announcement in a church bulletin spoke of celebrating the birth of "Patrick Alan Miller, the sin of Rev. and Mrs. Alden Miller."

47. Check dates against the calendar.

Make sure the day and date coincide. If you write "Monday, May 3," verify that May 3 is a Monday. I recently received an invitation where the day and date didn't match up. The person who sent the invitation was bombarded with phone calls. A few people didn't notice the discrepancy and showed up on the wrong day.

48. Print out the message and read from the hard copy.

No matter how proficient we may be at reading from the computer screen, we're still more accustomed to hard copy. When you print out your message, you may pick up errors you didn't see on the screen.

Create a disclaimer. I learned of a CFO who includes the following disclaimer at the end of her messages: "Please forgive any errors; I'm writing on a BlackBerry." Although it's

prudent always to be as accurate as you can, people have said
that they're more forgiving because of her disclaimer.

49. Edit for content.

Editing refers to amending text by modifying words, sentences,
paragraphs, or the general structure of the document. Here are
some editing guidelines:

- **Be sure your sentences and paragraphs flow smoothly.**

- **Sequence your document so it tells the story.** (Check out
  Tip 30 so you tell your story for the impact you want to
  have on your reader.)

- **Look for omissions—things you left out.** For example,
  did you remember to attach the document you mentioned in your email message?

- **Reword any sentences you have to read more than once.** If
  you have trouble with comprehension, the reader will also.

- **Read the document aloud.** Reading aloud, even in a
  mumble, will slow you down so you read what's there,
  rather than what you expect to see there.

- **Have someone else read it.** When a document is important, have someone else read it.

 Can you read your message just once and understand it
clearly? Or do you scratch your head, wrinkle your brow,
grimace, and start again? If it's the latter, rewrite the sentence,
paragraph, or message.

Before you hit "Send," reread your message. If you
wouldn't say it to the reader's face, don't send it.

Selecting Appropriate Options

One cool judgment is worth
a thousand hasty councils.

WOODROW WILSON

Stop to think carefully about the importance of your message and who must receive it.

50. Determine if you require a read receipt.

There are times you want to make sure someone receives your message. When you request a read receipt, a header appears on the recipient's email asking for a confirmation. (This feature is akin to asking the reader of a letter delivered by the post office to sign a return receipt.) When you get the confirmation, you know the recipient received your message.

> Remember to request a read receipt only for very important messages. People don't necessarily want to divulge when or if they've read every email they receive, and constant pop-ups demanding a response can be annoying. Before requesting a receipt, ask yourself if it's reasonable to expect one.

51. Know the people you should include.

Don't send emails to people who don't *need* to see them. Too often people use distribution lists inappropriately. If you need to send a message to three people on a distribution list of ten, delete the names of the seven people who don't *need* to see it.

52. Use *To:*, *Cc:*, and *Bcc:* appropriately.

When sending an email to multiple readers, always determine each reader's significance with regard to the message. Choose from the following options carefully because each has advantages and pitfalls.

To:	All the readers' names appear in the *To:* field of all the emails.
Use when . . .	• all readers are of equal importance. • it's critical for everyone to know who received the message.
Example:	A CEO sends a message to all his VPs.
Pitfalls:	• Too many names can be daunting and over-shadow the message, especially on a hand-held computer. • Everyone's email address is revealed (on the screen or through Properties). • Anyone viewing your list can harvest the names to use or sell.

Cc:	All the names in the *To:* and *Cc:* fields appear in all the readers' fields.
Use when . . .	• one person is your primary reader. • you want your primary reader to know of another person (or people) to whom you're sending a *carbon copy* or *courtesy copy*.
Example:	You send a message to an employee and want him to know you copied his supervisor.
Pitfalls:	• Everyone's email address is revealed (on the screen or through Properties). • Anyone viewing your list can harvest the names to use or sell.
Bcc:	Each reader sees only his name in the *To:* field. There's no indication that anyone else received the message.
Use when . . .	• you don't want the primary reader to know you're sending a *blind carbon copy* of the message to anyone else. • you have a large distribution list and you don't want too many names in the *To:* and *Cc:* fields. • you want to protect the privacy of your readers. • you want to prevent anyone from harvesting your list to use or sell.
Examples:	You send an announcement, newsletter, invitation, or other email to everyone on a mailing list.

Pitfalls:
- Some spam filters delete anything in a *Bcc:* field, so your email may not reach your intended reader.
- It may appear as if you're going behind readers' backs. (Imagine what your reaction would be if you found out that other people received a copy of the same message and you didn't know.)

 To alleviate any sense of impropriety, mention the names of other readers in the body of the email. Or, if you are deliberately going behind someone's back, make sure to explain that in the message to the primary reader.

 When sending a blind copy, put your own address in the *To:* field.

53. Signal the importance of your message.

Remember, what's important to you may not be important to your reader. Use the high, medium, or low priorities realistically.

- To let your reader know your message is informational, use *FYI* at the start of the subject line.

- Rather than using a subject line that shouts and gives no information ("Important! Read Immediately!"), consider getting to the core of your message ("Important: All cars in fire lane will be towed in 1 hour").

Using Proper Email Etiquette

Email technology is marching forward too fast
for social rules to keep up, leaving
correspondents to police themselves and
sometimes commit gaffes that would
make Miss Manners wince.

JEFFREY BLAIR
columnist

When Alexander Graham Bell invented the telephone in 1876, he never anticipated how profoundly it would change the way people think and communicate. It was a remarkable invention that soon became the centerpiece of the workplace. Like the telephone, email has continued to revolutionize the way people interact.

Email is the main stop on the information superhighway. It has replaced many of the letters and memos businesspeople used to write. But the ease of sending and receiving creates inherent problems. People have a tendency to prepare email messages on the fly and fire them off to everyone in the universe. Just because email is quick and easy, it shouldn't travel at the speed of thoughtlessness. Always use common sense!

54. Send one message for each topic.

I often hear participants in my workshops complain that readers don't answer their messages, or they send only partial answers. That's often because senders include too many topics in one email. Readers can't digest too many disparate thoughts. Here are a couple of suggestions:

- If your message contains several topics about a variety of issues, add an introductory line letting the reader know what's in the text.

- If the topics are substantial or disparate enough, split them into separate emails, and create an appropriate subject line for each.

55. Say hello and goodbye.

You say hello when you answer the telephone. You include *Dear [name]* when you write a letter. You also say goodbye when you end a telephone conversation and include a closing when you conclude a letter. The people who don't start emails with greetings or end with closings are the same ones who walk into a room and bark out orders before they remove their coats—somewhat like the domineering boss played by Meryl Streep in *The Devil Wears Prada*. Always include a salutation and closing in your emails. They don't have to be as formal as in a letter, but they should be included. Here are a few suggestions:

Salutations	Closings
Hi Margo,	See you later,
Hi Mr. Gordon:	Best wishes,
Hello everyone,	Thanks,
Hi,	Regards,
Denise,	Best regards,
Hi everyone,	Have a great weekend,
Good morning,	See you tomorrow,

Avoid closings such as *Yours truly* and *Sincerely* (too formal for email), *Cordially* (passé), *Later* (unless you're a teenager), *Cheers* (for close friends only), and *Ciao* (unless you're in Italy).

56. Include an electronic signature.

Prepare an electronic signature file that ends each message. (Check your software's Help screen if you don't know how.) This is akin to letterhead on stationery; it allows readers to contact you easily. It's also free advertising when you include a message about your company. Here's the electronic signature that concludes all my messages:

Sheryl Lindsell-Roberts, Principal
Sheryl Lindsell-Roberts & Associates
www.sherylwrites.com
sheryl@sherylwrites.com
508-229-8209

You make more dollars when you make more sense!™

If you mention in the text that you want someone to call you or check your website, be sure to include the reference at the point of mention—for example, "Please check my website, **www.sherylwrites.com**." Even though that information may be included in your signature block, readers don't necessarily look for it.

57. Never send a Rambogram.

A Rambogram is a message that's crude, rude, or lewd. The next time you're tempted to send a gruff, ill-tempered, or snippy email, pause, take a deep breath, and think again. You don't want to be like Attorney A in the following story (condensed from an article in *The Boston Globe*):

Attorney B was miffed when Attorney A notified him by email that she'd changed her mind about working at his law firm—after having accepted the position verbally. Here's the gist of the messages they exchanged:

Attorney A: The pay you are offering would neither fulfill me nor support the lifestyle I am living.

Attorney B: Your email smacks of immaturity and is quite unprofessional. After you accepted, I ordered stationery and business cards, reformatted your computer, and set up your email account. However, I sincerely wish you the best of luck in your future endeavors.

Attorney A: A real lawyer would have put the contract into writing.

Attorney B: Thank you for the refresher course on contracts. This is not a bar exam question. You need to realize that this is a very small legal community, especially the criminal defense bar. Do you really want to start pissing off more

experienced lawyers this early in your career?
Attorney A: bla bla bla.

Attorney B was so incensed that he started circulating the exchange of emails, which ultimately traveled around the country and across the Atlantic. As a result, Attorney A was blacklisted and is now working by herself in a space in Boston where she takes court-appointed cases. Was justice served?

58. Be savvy when it comes to privacy issues.

Email and privacy are mutually exclusive. Just as a pedestrian passing the mailbox outside your home can reach in and intercept your mail, hackers, criminals, company administrators, and the government can intercept your email. Also, you don't know what system your email is passing through or what system other people's emails are passing through.

Email has raised a lot of issues about privacy, and many cases have been brought before the courts. The Electronic Communications Privacy Act of 1986 upholds a company's right to monitor its email. (Check out Tips 104–106, "Creating a Company Policy.") So, it's prudent not to send anything that you wouldn't want posted on the company's bulletin board. Here are two cases in point:

- A large entertainment company was in the midst of bankruptcy proceedings. Vast numbers of files were confiscated. Among those files were incriminating email messages that weren't meant for the public eye. This led to the dismissal of several high-level executives.

- A noted New York columnist opened a bluntly critical email message from a young female colleague. He responded with a barrage of sexual and racial epithets that got him suspended for two weeks.

 Did you know that the government can monitor email messages for security purposes?

59. Respond promptly.

You always want to appear professional and courteous, so try to answer emails within 24 hours. If you aren't in a position to act on the message, you may reply with, "Sorry, I won't have that information until sometime next week. I'll send it to you once I receive it."

60. Post to your company's intranet, blog, or website.

When your message needs to reach large numbers of people, find alternatives to sending attachments. If a message is static (not likely to change) and is of interest to a wide range of people, post it to your company's intranet, blog, or website. Then send an email letting people know it's there. Include the link. This is a great way to share the details of the upcoming company picnic and other issues of interest to your colleagues.

Many companies have password-protected areas on their websites for messaging. Messaging is a good choice for information that needs to be regularly updated. For example, you might send a message to your San Francisco office listing the phone numbers of people in your Boston office. When people join the company, leave, or get reassigned, you can send an updated message so the information stays current.

61. Inform people of a change of address.

The comedian Rodney Dangerfield joked that when he was a young boy his parents sent him off to school one morning and when he arrived home, the house was empty. The furniture and the people were gone. His parents had moved and left no forwarding address.

Don't abandon your email colleagues in the same way. Whenever you change your email address (whether you have changed jobs or service providers), let those you correspond with know your new address. After all, when you move your office or change your phone number, you let people know.

62. Break the chain.

Chain letters and scams are rampant in the electronic world; they contribute dramatically to information overload. When you receive jokes, hoaxes, surveys, bogus warnings, recipes, huge financial rewards, petitions, cute clip art, and more, don't open them and don't pass them on.

63. Determine whether to reply to all or just to the sender.

An HR director sent invitations to the company holiday party to 150 employees requesting an RSVP. Most employees replied to all, when only the HR director needed the head count. Respond to everyone when everyone needs to see your answer; otherwise, respond only to the sender.

64. Reserve "urgent" for pressing messages.

There are people who designate all their messages "urgent" or "priority." (We all know who they are.) I can recall instances when I didn't respond to a truly urgent message because the sender was the little boy who cried wolf. Following are a few pieces of advice for wolf criers:

- Unless a message is truly urgent, don't tag it as such.

- If you must get the message through as quickly as possible, consider phoning rather than emailing and risking that the recipient won't see the message in time. People are more likely to listen to phone messages than read email messages. (Check out Tip 1.)

- If a message is merely informational, consider starting the subject line with *FYI*. People will begin to recognize that notation as a clue to read the message when they get around to it.

E-Marketing

*Industry average response rates are 5–15%
for e-mail, 1–2% for direct mail, and .055–1%
for banner advertising.*

JUNIPER COMMUNICATIONS

Electronic marketing (e-marketing) is one of the communications marvels of the century. It builds relationships and creates top-of-the-mind awareness with your customers and clients. E-marketing is fast and cost-effective, and its results are measurable. It can also be customized to a specific market or markets. You can use e-marketing for special offers, tips, HTMLs, PDF files, coupons, newsletters, and more.

Remember that if you abuse e-marketing, you may damage your reputation and violate federal law. Any e-marketing message you send should identify the person/company sending the message and should clearly pinpoint the offer. It should also provide the right to opt out. (Check out Tip 75.)

 On pages 71–73 you'll find *After* and *Before* emails that demonstrate many of the tips in this section.

65. Try a "top 10."

The success of your e-marketing campaign hinges on just a few words—the subject line. You don't have to be the company bard waiting for a visit from the marketing muse to write a compelling subject line. Be insightful, think *in*side the box, and don't use the same subject line for more than one campaign.

Studies show that "top 10" subject lines are winners. When you're stuck for a subject line, pull a "top 10" from your bag of tricks. Add your name to enhance branding.

> Paula's top 10 best resources for . . .
> Jon's top 10 reasons why . . .
> CEOs share top 10 reasons for . . .

66. Include a call to action or a sense of urgency.

When you include a call to action and create a sense of urgency, you compel the reader to open your message and act immediately.

> Get 50% off—register by March 3
> Reply by June 5. Seating is limited
> Special pre-release offer good through May 16. Call today

67. Use statistics or numbers.

When you use statistics or numbers, be sure they're from reliable research or resources. This adds credibility to what you're marketing. And enhance the statistic with a pitch that will encourage curiosity.

> 75% of new businesses will fail. Beat the odds
> Discover in just 5 days what . . .
> Use for 30 days at no cost . . .

Engage the reader with a question.

Can 5,000 CEOs be wrong?
Have you ever considered ... ?
When was the last time you ... ?

68. Test the word *free*.

Yes, it's true that spam looks for the word *free*, but it's a word that continues to get people's attention when it does get through. Don't use *fr*e, f ree, freee,* or any variation of the word; it will stand out as spam like a wart on the end of your nose. Also, consider some variations such as *at no cost, complimentary, without charge:*

> Free Kit: Maximize profits in just six months
> Analysis of your telephone & Internet bills at no charge

Compose at least four or five subject lines before deciding which to use. Select the two best and test them against each other.

69. Personalize the message for your target audience.

Once the subject line has lured your readers into opening your message, the message must be enticing. In 2002, *eMail Marketing Weekly* conducted a survey to determine how important it is to personalize your message to reflect your reader's name, interests, gender, age, purchase history, and message frequency preferences. The results found that nonpersonalized bulk emails got a 4.7 percent response rate, and personalized bulk emails got a 14.8 percent response rate. To personalize your message, ask these questions:

- What does your target audience want, need, or respond to?

- What frustrates them?

- Who is your competition?

- Why should your audience respond to you instead of to someone else?

- What makes you credible?

An instant way to personalize your message is to open with the person's name (*Dear Mr. Banks:*) and end with a sincere closing.

70. Offer something the reader will value.

For a high opt-in rate, make sure you send readers something they'll value. It may be a business-related tip, industry update, or timely article. Don't send a self-serving message about your company's latest products or services. If your message is perceived as sales-y or fluffy, your reader will dismiss it immediately and you will lose credibility.

Jot down the benefits and features of your product or service. *Benefits* appeal to a person's emotional needs: Increased revenue, a more stylish look, a better quality of life, a decrease in production time, a shorter assembly time, or a doubled yield are examples of benefits. *Features* are the attributes of a product or service: Densely packed multi-chip modules, lead generation selection and qualification approval, or a sales account diary for storing notes about clients are examples of features.

People typically make purchases based on emotion. When you appeal to curiosity, greed, ego, narcissism, hope, fear, or security, you make an emotional appeal.

71. Speak your reader's language.

If you're writing to people in a specific industry, use jargon they understand. If your message is going to an international audience, know how your English message will translate. According to urban legend, when Coca-Cola came to China, the first people who sold the drink had to choose characters to represent the name. Unfortunately the characters they picked could be interpreted as meaning "bite the wax tadpole." And when Chevrolet introduced the Nova, they found that *no va* means "no go" in Spanish.

72. Grab the reader's attention quickly.

Grab the reader's attention in the first sentence and again in the last sentence. Consider making the last sentence a postscript. In that way you capture the attention of people who read the first few lines then skip to the end.

73. Use tried-and-tested phrases.

Here are some words and phrases in messages that have been shown to spark interest:

Congratulations! You're our 10th winner.
Forgive me, for I have spammed.
Here's your discount.
Alert!
Limited time only.
Success
Look at this only if you . . .

74. Include a call to action.

Take your reader by the hand and tell him exactly what you want him to do. Make your call to action clear, compelling, rewarding, and urgent. Perhaps you want your reader to click on a link, call you, download an e-book, buy tickets, make a donation, place an order, sign up for a service, or fill out a form. Include compelling phrases such as *Try this for 60 days before deciding to buy* or *The first 100 customers* . . . Pepper your message with the call to action so the reader can click whenever he's ready.

Consider including the call to action at the beginning of the message to make sure the reader doesn't miss it. (Check out the *After* message on pages 71-72.)

75. Let the reader opt in or opt out.

Spam is in the eyes of the beholder. Some people appreciate information about products and services that can enhance their business or personal lives. Others see such information as an invasion of privacy. As long as you give people the ability to opt out, you're covered. Following are a few examples of how to let people opt out:

> We respect your privacy. If you want to be removed from this list, <u>click here</u> to opt out and we'll remove your name immediately.

> To opt out, <u>click here</u>.

When you have a list of people who opt in, perhaps they'd be interested in other products or services that relate to them. Here's how I've asked that of the associates on my opt-in list:

> We work with several partners whose products and services we recommend. Would you be interested in receiving information from them? Please <u>opt in</u> or <u>opt out</u>. Thank you.

Timing is everything. Send your e-marketing messages so the recipient receives them during the workday. Everyone has a full inbox early in the morning, so your message may get lost in the shuffle. At the end of the day, people are anxious to leave.

76. Know when to send.

Conventional wisdom says you should send business-to-business (B2B) messages midweek, on Tuesdays, Wednesdays, or Thursdays. Mondays are considered "pile-up" days when people return from the weekend. On Fridays, people are often eager to leave the office to start the weekend.

If you send e-messages on Mondays or Fridays, turn them into positives:

Start the week off right.
Start the weekend off right.
End the week right.

Test your campaign. Testing will assure your highest response rate. Test only one variable at a time so that you can easily tell which variable made the difference.

77. Test your list, offer, body copy, call to action, delivery day, and delivery time.

If you have a low open rate, take a look at your subject line:

- Is it short and to the point?

- Does it mention a specific benefit?

- Does it look like spam?

- Was your delivery date and/or time appropriate?

If you have a low click-through rate, consider the following:

- **Your call to action.** Is your call to action clear? Do you make it easy for recipients to answer your call to action by putting links throughout your email? Do your links work?

- **Your copy.** Are you writing to your target audience? Is your text clear and concise? Are the benefits of the offer right up front?

- **Your offer.** Does your offer fulfill the promise of your subject line? Is your product or service too expensive? Have you created a sense of urgency with a time limit?

78. Don't give up.

Whatever you do, don't give up because of less-than-stellar results the first few times. If more than 5 percent of your subscribers opt out regularly, take a look at all of the elements of your campaigns and make adjustments. Ask a few customers with whom you have a close relationship why they unsubscribed. Take immediate action based on their comments.

Consider using a blog as part of your online marketing efforts. Ed Brill, an IBMer, says, "As a sales/marketing leader, being able to have an intimate one-to-one relationship with thousands of customers who buy/deploy/manage the product I sell is immensely rewarding. . . . I have been able to win business, save business, and affect the market and competitive landscape through blogging." (Check out Tips 128–131, "Capitalizing on the Value of Blogs.")

Build a list of associates—people with whom you do business, people you've met with whom you'd like to do business, and people who can help you grow your business. Get their email addresses, and use email as a touchpoint for sending things of interest to your readers. This can be a newsletter, an article you came across, a website of interest, and more.

* * *

Following are two different versions of the same e-marketing message. The *Before* example has a dull subject line, and the key information is buried. The *After* example has a compelling subject line, and the key information jumps out. Notice how the *After* example . . .

- entices the readers with an attention-grabbing subject line.

- offers something of value.

- personalizes the message by adding *Dear Mr. Baxter* and ending with *Best regards* above a signature block.

- grabs the reader's attention quickly with a call to action in the first line.

- points to key information with *topic, date, time,* and *registration deadline* clearly called out.

- gets to the point.

- stresses key information with bold and underscore.

- includes lots of white space around key information.

- offers the ability to opt out.

- includes an electronic signature.

E-Marketing Message (**After**)

To:	Brian Baxter
Subject:	Mistakes CIOs make in their first 90 days: Learn to avoid them.

Dear Mr. Baxter:

Please call me at 508-229-8209 to participate in this enlightening teleseminar to help you on the success track starting from day one. It's the first 90 days on the job that can make or break your career. This teleseminar is not to be missed; your career may depend on it.

> **Topic: Mistakes CIOs make in their first 90 days: Learn to avoid them.**
> **Date:** April 1, 20—
> **Time:** 1:00–2:00

> **Registration deadline: March 15, 20—**

I participated in this teleseminar in January 20— and learned lots of valuable information. I now feel I'm much better equipped to lead the team at my company and am on a fast-success track.
--Brooke Riley, CIO, Marric Technologies, Inc.

Best regards,
Sheryl Lindsell-Roberts

Sheryl Lindsell-Roberts, Principal
Sheryl Lindsell-Roberts & Associates
sheryl@sheryl writes.com
http://www.sherylwrites.com
508-229-8209

We respect your privacy. If you want to be removed from this list, click here to opt out and we'll remove your name immediately.

E-Marketing Message (**Before**)

To: Brian Baxter
Subject: Teleseminar for CIOs and CTOs

As you know, many CIOs have trouble in the first 90 days on the job, a period which can make or break their careers. *CIO* magazine is always interested in helping our members, and we invite you to participate in a teleseminar entitled Mistakes CIOs make in their first 90 days. It will be on April 1 from 1:00 to 2:00. This teleseminar is one of the best you'll ever phone into. The deadline to register is March 15, so please call us today at 508-123-4567 to participate in this enlightening teleseminar. Put April 1 on your calendar. You'll be glad you did.

I participated in this teleseminar in January 20— and learned lots of valuable information. I now feel I'm much better equipped to lead the team at my company and am on a fast-success track.

--Brooke Riley, CIO
  Marric Technologies, Inc.

Managing Time Efficiently

*I'm definitely going to take a course on
time management ... just as soon as I can
work it into my schedule.*

LOUIS E. BOONE
American educator and business writer

Studies show that employees spend about 2 hours a day sending and reading email, much of which is of little importance. Do the math. That's 10 hours a week, 40 hours a month, and 480 hours a year. Imagine what you could you do with an additional 480 hours each year. If email is killing your productivity, here are some guidelines to turn your email into a dynamic business tool.

79. Use filters to battle spam and other unwanted messages.

You can set up filters to handle spam and unwanted messages so that you manage your email rather than have it manage you. If you have Microsoft Outlook Express, for example, go to the Tools menu, point to Message Rules, click Block Senders List, and click the name or domain you want to remove.

 Have you ever wondered where spam comes from? If you place your email on a website, spammers use harvesting programs to grab your address. They grab your email address from open chatrooms. They create "guessed names" to see if your message bounces back. And, like it or not, when you place an order online, businesses sell your email address to other businesses. The Federal Trade Commission has passed many anti-spam regulations, but spammers are rarely caught. The best way to combat spam is to invest in a good spam program or have one email account dedicated to activities outside the business arena.

80. Turn off your announcement feature.

The telephone rings when the caller wants it to—often during inappropriate times. With email, you can control your "rings." When you check email on demand, you become its victim. Turn off the automatic announcement feature on your email and check it at your convenience.

81. Develop a schedule for checking your email.

Whether you get a few emails each day or hundreds, very few need immediate attention. (If they do, the sender should have called instead of sending an email.) Develop a schedule for checking email, but don't check it during your most productive or creative hours.

82. Choose the way you want to view your email.

Most programs offer several viewing options such as by sender, by subject, by date. You can also opt to have unread messages highlighted or you can use the preview option to get a glimpse of the first few lines.

83. Organize your messages into folders.

Do you clutter your metal file cabinets with papers that have no order? Probably not. You categorize the papers and place them in labeled file folders so you can retrieve them easily. Rather than keeping your emails in your inbox, create e-file folders and label them as you do paper folders.

Organize by file types and give each file a logical, plain-language name. You want to be able to identify each folder without having to open it. (If you look back a year later, will you remember what TCB means?) Nest folders within main folders and label accordingly. For example, you might use "Billing 2006, 2007, 2008, 2009."

84. Don't leave email sitting in your inbox.

Once you open a message, synthesize it and take some kind of action:

- Delete whatever you're absolutely certain you'll never need again.

- Create a folder labeled "Old" or "Inactive" for anything you're unsure about.

- Move the message to a folder.

- Add the item to your to-do list.
- Add the date to your calendar.
- Forward the message to someone who *needs* to see it.

85. Create a work-life balance.

Technology was supposed to free us, not tether us. Many people don't leave email at the office. They check messages at home into the wee hour of the night or morning. They check email while on vacation. They check email while on the golf course.

If you're "e-dicted" to your email, determine times that are off limits. For example, don't think about email between dinner and the children's bedtimes. Schedule small amounts of time while on vacation to check your messages (if you must).

86. Don't use email as a substitute for a conversation.

Know when email is and isn't appropriate. Always ask yourself if another form of communication would be more expedient. (Check out Tip 1.)

Help your reader with time management. When sending a message, make your action item clear in the first sentence or two. If you mention the action item at the end, the reader may not page down far enough to see it, especially if he's using a PDA. Here's an example with the action item at the beginning: "Please send me the report by close of business on May 5. Following are the details."

Communicating with Teams

*Treat people as if they were what they
ought to be and you help them to become
what they are capable of being.*

JOHANN WOLFGANG VON GOETHE
German poet and dramatist

Email is the cornerstone of communication for most teams, whether they're co-located or remotely located. Yet surprisingly few teams have created agreed-upon email standards that inspire the disciplines they need to save time and frustration. It is critical that remote teams have well-articulated email practices because there are few opportunities to address communication misfires.

As more of us scan our emails in parallel with other activities, it's especially important to create emails that get the results we want in the shortest time. We need to help other team members focus on our most important issues. If you're having trouble keeping up with the fusillade of emails your team members churn out each day or you're wondering why team members don't respond to your messages, the tips in this section may help.

This is the true account of a poorly written email that caused a company to lose a major client. Pete (I changed his name to protect the guilty) was the team leader for a large project. If this project was successful, Pete's company was going to acquire one of its largest customers. One morning something happened that threatened the success of the project. Several high-level people needed to take immediate action.

Here's what Pete did and didn't do. He . . .

- sent an email to the three high-level people letting them know what they needed to do.
- used the same subject line he used for his weekly reports, which was the name of the project.
- started the message (which spanned four screens) with background information about the project.
- communicated the problem on the second screen.
- didn't flag the message as "urgent" or "priority."
- didn't mention the action items early—he waited until the end of the fourth screen.
- didn't follow up to make sure the intended recipients read his message.

None of the intended recipients read Pete's email; therefore, none took action. Even if they had read the message, Pete didn't lead off with the problem or the action they needed to take. As a result of Pete's email incompetence, his company lost this potential customer.

What should Pete have done? He should have . . .

- called instead of sending an email. Or, he should have requested a read receipt to make sure his message was read. If he didn't get the receipt, he would have known to follow up with a call.
- flagged the message as "urgent" or "priority."
- created a compelling subject line such as, "Problem needing IMMEDIATE action."

■ started the text portion of the message as follows: "As a result of [incident] that happened this morning, each of you must take these immediate actions."

87. Determine when and how email will be used by the team.

Email tends to be the default method of communicating, so having a plan is especially critical when a team is geographically dispersed. Remember that email is not always the most efficient or effective way to get messages across. It may be more appropriate for some members or some phases of a team's work than others. There may be better options, depending on your objectives and intended audience. (Check out Tip 1.)

Take the time to agree as a team under what conditions email is best, and in what situations another communication channel may work better. As an alternative to email, consider posting your documents on the team's intranet site or creating a blog. When you do, make sure people know when new information is posted and provide the links.

88. Decide between mass distribution and selective sending.

Avoid the temptation to cover all the bases by routinely sending or copying everyone on every email. For example, determine in advance who ...

■ needs to be included in the *To:* list on your status report.

■ needs to be copied.

■ doesn't need to know.

Also agree on whether you'll be using *Bcc*. Some people find *Bcc:* disconcerting. Check in with team members from time to time to validate your assumptions about their wanting to be included or excluded on emails about certain topics. Until you're certain, err on the side of over-communicating, especially with a new team when relationships are still being formed.

89. Establish standards for response time.

Be aware of people's vacation schedules and holidays in other countries. And remember that not everyone is willing to interrupt a vacation just because you've marked an email "urgent." If team members work in a variety of time zones, try setting a standard by which they can respond to email requests by the end of their business day. In this way colleagues working behind them have what they need at the start of *their* day. Create conventions to signify urgency in the header so you flag the level of priority.

90. Create a subject line that is clear, concise, and informative.

Type your main message in the subject line. (Check out Tips 24–27, "Crafting a Compelling Subject Line.") In that way, someone can grasp the gist without having to open your message. Use strong words to grab your reader's attention.

For example, if your project is in trouble, instead of writing "Project status" as your subject, write "Project threatened by lack of funding." This will ensure that readers will be motivated to read the text. It's also easier to file the message and access it later when the subject line reflects the content of the message.

91. Call the reader's attention to actions, issues, and decisions by calling them out in headlines.

The first few lines of an email are critical because they may be the only ones read, especially if your reader accesses email from a PDA. For example, if adherence to ground rules is important to the success of a meeting, call that out right up front in your meeting email. You might say, "Please arrange your calendars to ensure that we have 60 minutes of your undivided attention for this call. Multitasking will not allow the kind of valuable contributions we need from each of you."

Underline key words in red, make them boldface, or otherwise highlight them. Headlines may include <u>Action Requested</u>, <u>Next Step</u>, or anything else that is appropriate.

92. Understand the questions your reader will have by asking yourself *who, what, when, where, why*, and *how*.

Before you compose your message, consider what questions your reader will need answered. (Check out Tips 21 and 22.) Condense that information into the first few sentences, as in this example:

First drafts of FY '08 budget plans are due to cost center managers by November 15. All plans must be in Excel format, using the FINPLAN07 budget planning template found in the first entry of our SharePoint directory under the topic "Budgets and plans." You can find an example of a completed plan in the document named SAMPLEPLAN 08, listed as the second entry in this same location.

By providing all the necessary information up front, you will avoid potential questions later.

93. Anticipate your reader's likely reaction in order to defuse negativity.

If your message is likely to be sensitive, contentious, or met with resistance, test the message and subject line with someone else first. With a virtual team, you have very few opportunities to make amends if you offend or upset someone via email.

When you deliver negative news, try to offer options or provide a rationale so that people can be understanding. (Check out Tip 30.) For example, if you're letting someone know that you cannot complete a report by next Monday, consider mentioning that you can have the first two critical sections by Monday.

Remember, if you're delivering negative news, either call or discuss it face to face. Then follow up with email as confirmation.

94. Eliminate all words and thoughts that don't add value, while being personable and complete.

It's much easier for many of us to spew out as many details as we can think of, leaving our harried readers to extract the hidden kernels. It may require more thought to hone your key message, but ultimately you'll save time by avoiding unnecessary follow-up calls, emails, and IMs. When you write an email of substantial length or substance, compose it on your word processor. In this way, you can edit and save the draft for later, rather than feel compelled to hit "Send" before you've had a chance to revise it and proofread it.

95. Proofread very carefully.

Eliminating typos is relatively easy when you use a spell checker. However, many words have valid spellings that you may have used incorrectly (*complement* and *compliment*, for example). Also reread for grammar, clarity, flow, and organization. If you question whether you've used a tone that may be offensive, test it with others.

96. Develop cultural sensitivity.

Following are some suggestions for sending messages to team members from other countries and cultures. (Check out Tip 6 for more details.)

- Test important messages with people who understand both cultures.

- Make sure your tone is appropriate and your content is clear.

- Err on the side of formality, especially with new team members who may chafe at a casual salutation or be perplexed by your attempts at humor.

- Minimize abbreviations and acronyms. (If you must use them, explain them.)

- Avoid slang and jargon.

- Use simple vocabulary and conventional syntax.

- Over-explain, rather than under-explain.

- Address people by their last names, unless you know them well enough to call them by their first names. People of other cultures tend to be more formal than Americans.

97. Check back in with people.

Take the time to check in with people on the phone after they've received important emails. This ensures that there are no misunderstandings. (This advice would have helped poor Pete, the subject of the Word from Sheryl on page 78.)

Understanding Legal Implications

[Twenty-four percent of employers have] had employee email subpoenaed in the course of a lawsuit or regulatory investigation. That's more than double the 9% reported in 2001, and a 4% increase over the 20% reported in 2004. Another 15% have battled workplace lawsuits triggered by employee email. Yet, in spite of the fact that email and instant messages are a primary source of evidence—the electronic equivalent of DNA evidence—employers remain largely ill-prepared to manage email and instant messaging risks.

NANCY FLYNN
author and executive director,
The ePolicy Institute

Email leaves a permanent trail, as shown by the statistics cited above from the *2006 Workplace E-Mail, Instant Messaging & Blog Survey,* a study of 416 companies conducted by the American Management Association and The ePolicy Institute. The trail resides not only on your computer and the recipient's computer, but on several servers in between. Miscommunicate and any Machiavellian scheming behind your back may throw your email in your face. There are thousands of stories to demonstrate this. Here are just two:

- In a small New Jersey town, the police seized the email of a murder suspect in the investigation of a homicide case. On the strength of evidence that included incriminating emails, the man was charged with murder.

- A hapless email user wanted to send a romantic, risqué love letter to his girlfriend. He inadvertently sent the letter to 100 shocked coworkers as well. Romeo immediately realized what he'd done and called the provider to retrieve the message. His service didn't have "Unsend" capabilities.

The "Unsend" feature (if your system has one) is unpredictable at best. For example, if your network runs Microsoft Exchange Server, you can recall an email that's unread if the exchange server is in the same network or the same company as yours and the recipient's. You would have the choice of deleting the unread copy of the message or deleting the unread copy and replacing it with a new message. There's also a box that tells you if the recall succeeded or failed. More often than not, if the message was sent to someone outside your company, the cat may already be out of the bag. It's best to be sure you want to send the message before you hit the "Send" key.

98. Know the proper and lawful use of company email.

According to Jean Sifleet, business attorney, CPA, and author, "Many companies think that having an email policy is enough to protect them from legal exposure. That's just not realistic.

Employees use email for all sorts of activities, and they need to be trained about what's okay and what's not okay."

> An exchange of emails can result in a legally binding contract. You want to be clear about the terms before you hit "Send" and make a legal commitment. Be on the lookout for a misplaced decimal point, an omitted word, or anything else that may have dire consequences.

99. Remember that libel and copyright laws apply to email.

Most people wouldn't steal someone's wallet, but the same people who wouldn't steal a wallet may use the Internet as a license to copy intellectual property, software, images, songs, and more. Email documents are subject to the same libel and copyright laws as paper-based documents. For example, you can't copy an article from an online newspaper or magazine and paste it into an email unless you get permission from the publisher. If the text you're copying is short (just a few sentences), you can include the reference without formally obtaining permission, but you must give credit to the source.

100. Become familiar with the Sarbanes-Oxley Act.

The Sarbanes-Oxley Act, affectionately known as SOX (not to be confused with the Boston Red Sox or Chicago White Sox) was enacted in 2002 following the Enron and WorldCom scandals. Because most organizations use email to exchange messages and documents, SOX mandates how long and in what manner email should be retained. For more information check out **http://www.soxlaw.com**.

101. Avoid anything that could be construed as sexual harassment.

Sexual harassment goes beyond requests for sexual favors, unwelcome sexual advances, or verbal or physical conduct that's offensive. Check your company's policy. Here's a case in point:

> Grace was the new office manager of a large company. Her first day on the job, John sent an email to Paul saying he thought Grace was "hot." Over the next several weeks John and Paul exchanged emails about Grace. The messages got more and more descriptive and began to include body parts the guys found particularly attractive. They failed to realize the company was monitoring their email. Even though neither one of them ever spoke a word to Grace, they were brought up on sexual harassment charges. They got off with a warning, but their employment records were blemished.

102. Include a disclaimer at the end of your email, if appropriate.

You can sometimes minimize legal risks when you add a disclaimer or confidential notice to every email sent from your network. A disclaimer may read as follows:

> Confidentiality Notice: This email message, including any attachments, is intended for the sole use of the

designated recipient(s). It may contain confidential or proprietary information and may be protected by legal, professional, or other privilege. Any unauthorized review, use, duplication, forwarding, disclosure, or distribution is prohibited. If you are not the designated recipient, you are hereby notified that reading, disseminating, disclosing, distributing, copying, forwarding, acting upon, or otherwise using the information contained in this email is strictly prohibited. If you have received this email in error, please notify the sender as soon as possible and delete this message.

 Check out **http://www.emaildisclaimers.com**, which is chock-full of information about disclaimers.

103. Abide by the CAN-SPAM Act.

The CAN-SPAM (Controlling the Assault of Non-Solicited Pornography and Marketing) Act of 2003 established regulations for sending unsolicited commercial email. Here's a brief summary of the law's requirements:

- Within 10 days you must honor someone's request to be removed from your distribution list.

- You must include a physical address in the message, even if it's a post office box. This address must remain active for 30 days after you send the email.

- You cannot use a misleading subject line.

- You must clearly label sexually oriented messages in the subject line (although only perverts send them).

- You cannot use headlines containing false information.

- You must include opt-out instructions.

- You cannot sell your opt-out list for others to spam.

The Coalition Against Unsolicited Commercial Email (CAUCE) is promoting legislation in the United States and Europe that would make it illegal to send any unsolicited commercial email unless the sender and the recipient have an existing business relationship. These laws would protect Internet users from spam the way do-not-call lists protect consumers from telemarketers. Check out these websites for the latest federal regulations:

Federal Rules of Civil Procedure
http://www.inboxer.com/downloads/Whitepaper_FRCP.pdf

HIPPA
http://www.ciphersend.com/hipaa.html

FCC CAN-SPAM Wireless
http://www.emaillabs.com/email_marketing_articles/
FCC_CAN-SPAM_Wireless_Regulations.html

Creating a Company Policy

A man watches himself best when
others watch him too.

GEORGE SAVILE,
FIRST MARQUIS OF HALIFAX
English politician and essayist

Businesses today face a number of email threats that include breach of confidentiality, legal liability, damage to reputation, lost productivity, network congestion, and down time. Also, email can be retrieved if your company is facing a lawsuit. It's imperative that every company has, distributes, and updates a policy governing email. According to Nancy Flynn of The ePolicy Institute, "If you have a policy in place, have conducted a formal training program and have installed the proper technology, you can walk into a courtroom and demonstrate that you've done due diligence."

> Be sure your policy addresses other forms of electronic technology besides email, such as instant messages, text messages, blogs, and chats. Let employees know what is and isn't allowed.

104. Know what to include.

Here are some topics to address in a company policy:

Privacy and monitoring	The 1986 Electronic Communications Privacy Act allows employers to monitor employees via email as well as the telephone. Set up a monitoring procedure for outgoing and incoming email. Remind employees that email is a company asset, and they should not assume that any messages they send or receive are private. Explain whether monitoring is done systematically, only for business purposes, only with good cause, or whatever.
Wrongful and illegal purposes	As basic as this may be, it's necessary to state that company email may not be used for wrongful or illegal purposes and that electronic eavesdropping is prohibited.
Personal email *(See the Reminder on page 95.)*	Outline what is and isn't allowed for personal use. For example, you might allow employees to email spouses, children, partners, and other close family members during lunch or work breaks. However, you might not to allow them to use email to find another job, seek money for personal gain, promote personal causes, and the like.
Encryption and labeling	What encryption is allowed? Must employees label personal email as such? Determine if employees may use email for confidential information. If so, establish procedures for encryption and labeling.
Waste of resources	Include guidelines for the use of newsletters, newsgroups, and other non-business usage that may tie up network traffic.

Content	Explain that email must not contain offensive or disruptive content, must not discuss mergers or acquisitions, must not violate copyright infringement, must not disclose confidential company information, and the like.
Harassment	Remind employees that email must not contain jokes or inappropriate comments about a person's race, gender, age, sexual orientation, religion, political beliefs, national origin, or disability. It must not contain profane or obscene language or unprofessional remarks.
Retention	Some industries (such as the government, health care, and financial institutions) are required by law to archive electronic messages. Whether or not your industry is subject to such regulations, make it clear to employees which emails must be saved and archived and for how long.
Disclaimers	If disclaimers must appear in every email, state the exact text to be used. (Check out Tip 102.)
Passwords and security	Tell employees that they should not share their passwords with anyone, including their managers. The only exception to this rule is when the service desk is troubleshooting an issue and the employee's login credentials are needed. Once the issue has been resolved, the employee should change his password so he is the only one with knowledge of it.

Etiquette	Encourage employees to compose emails as courteously and professionally as they would a written document. Remind them that emails can be re-created long after they have been deleted from the employee's computer.
Violations	Outline the penalties for violating any or all of the policies.

Under laws administered by the National Labor Relations Board (NLRB), employers can't blanketly forbid employees from discussing issues involving their employment over email. However, if employees use email to interfere with business operations they may face dismissal. Here are two cases in point cited in "Email Use at Work—Rules of the Road," an article by Jean Sifleet, Mary C. Casey, and Susan P. Joyce:

Protected email Employee email was found to be a protected, concerted activity in *Timekeeping Systems, Inc. 323 NLRB No. 30* (Feb. 27, 1997). Discharge of an employee for his email response to employer's email notice about changes in the company's bonus and vacation policy, which was broadly distributed throughout the company, was found to be unlawful.

Unprotected email Employee email was found to be unprotected in *Washington Adventist Hospital, 291 NLRB 95* (1988). Employee sent a "break message" to 100 computer terminals in an acute care hospital, disrupting operations.

105. Publish and enforce.

Hand out hard copies of the policies to all employees, and ask employees to sign and date them. This will serve as an acknowledgment that they have read the policies and understand the consequences of not adhering to them. Policies should also be easily accessible in employee handbooks and/or on the company intranet. Some companies include the policies in employment contracts and ask new hires to acknowledge in writing that they've read them.

Provide training and take prompt action if policies are violated. Unless an employee comes forward with a complaint, the only way to know if the policies are being violated is though a monitoring system.

 Products such as InBoxer and OutBoxer can stop messages that violate company policy before they become a problem. For more information check out the following links:

http://www.inboxer.com
http://www.inboxer.com/prod_outboxer.shtml

106. Update as appropriate.

Update your company policies as new processes and new technologies surface. Include guidelines for instant messages, text messages, blogs, chatrooms, and any other technology that impacts your business. Out-of-date policies are liabilities, not assets.

 Telecommuters are subject to the same rules when working at home as they are when working in the office.

PART TWO

Instant Messages (IMs)

Instant messaging (IM or IMing)—the text version of a phone call—is becoming one of the most thriving colonies in the vast digital wilderness. It allows two or more Internet users to exchange text messages in a private chat. Considered the antithesis of formal communication, IM has some educators worried. Jeff Stanton, an associate professor at Syracuse University's School of Information Studies, received the following message from one of his students: "hi prof how r u culd u tell me my xm grade - tim."

"I am concerned [students] won't be successful if they don't know how to communicate on a formal basis," said Stanton. "The first time they send a goofy message to the boss, they're going to be out." Yet many experts believe that IM will eventually replace email as a key tool in business communications. Do you think IM is the wave of the future?

Look at what high school students are saying, and judge for yourself:

"IM language has become so ubiquitous, I don't realize I've lapsed into it."

"It's just natural. I have to learn not to do it in school."

"I was scrambling to finish an essay on my English final and accidentally put *b/c* instead of *because*."

Studies show that about one-third of Americans in their teens and twenties use IM as their primary channel for communicating. (They feel email is for "old fogies.") Check out these examples of IM's growing popularity:

▪ Many restaurants and retail stores are "getting the message" by taking orders and answering questions via IM. They claim to be seeing an increase in business.

- Technical call centers are using IM to "chat" with customers. The IM chat can be saved, so there's a permanent record of the interaction that can be used by others in the company to serve customers better. Prior to the advent of this technology, calls were recorded and call center employees had to type the conversation into a database.

- Many customer service centers rely on IM's "presence awareness," which means you can check who's active in the company's IM service. A typical scenario may be the following: A customer calls about the status of a purchase. You send an IM to someone in the appropriate department who's logged on, and you can give your customer an immediate answer. This eliminates having to track down the right person and get back to your customer. Therefore, you've satisfied your customer's needs on the spot.

- Call centers for health care providers also rely on IM, allowing nurses to work from home. When you call your doctor in the middle of the night, a nurse can answer the phone, fire off an IM to the doctor on duty, and get an expert response while the patient is still on the phone.

- Large retail outlets are blending web retailing and IM for a significant boost in sales. As reported by Davide Dukcevich, "Instant messaging has bolstered Lands' End's Web success. The company says that the average value of an order increases by 6% when a surfer uses its instant message technology. An online visitor who uses Lands' End's IM is 20% more likely to make a purchase than a customer who does not." (Forbes.com, July 22, 2007)

Several large financial institutions have taken a sledge-hammer approach and banned IM because they fear it will breed liability. In December 2006, five broker dealers were fined $8.5 million by the SEC, the NASD, and the New York Stock Exchange for failing to archive and retain records of IM conversations. Rather than banning IM completely, other institutions are allowing it in selected departments.

Implementing IM Safety Standards

*Instant messaging isn't just a new technology,
it's a new language. One that's especially easy
to over rely on, misinterpret and misuse.*

TOM VAN RIPER
"New Technologies Mean Adjustments for
Co-Workers of All Ages,"
Forbes, August 30, 2006

No longer a clandestine code of teenagers, IM is real-time communication facilitated by special software. IM is available for mobile devices such as smartphones as well as desktop and laptop computers. Text-based IM messages are immediately displayed on the screens of the recipients, and the messages of everyone participating are visible in sequence. IM also allows the user to attach files (photos, music, or whatever) or engage in video chats if both parties have a webcam. Popular software includes AIM (AOL Instant Messenger), ICQ, Apple's iChat, Yahoo! Messenger, MSN Messenger, Skype Instant Messenger—and the list continues to grow. IM is efficient because it eliminates the lag time of email and the chitchat of phone calls. Its use in business is expected to triple within the next several years.

107. Create company policies.

It's prudent to have a policy that covers all the communications technologies your company uses. (Check out Tips 104–106, "Creating a Company Policy.") From a legal perspective, there is no distinction between email and IM, yet many companies that monitor and archive email neglect IM.

Monte Enbysk, a lead editor for the Microsoft.com network, states, "Any policy should contain at least general guidelines for its use. You may not think this is a big deal—unless you know the story a few years ago about the San Francisco hedge fund manager who caused a major flap by allegedly using IM to spread inaccurate rumors about a publicly traded software company. (Word got out, the software company's stock plunged, and the hedge fund manager and his company got into some hot water.)"

108. Know which IM programs are on your network.

Free consumer IM programs are popular but often aren't secure. If employees have downloaded free IM programs (and at least half have, according to Nancy Flynn of The ePolicy Institute), you need to know about it. Nancy recommends surveying employees to learn which IM programs they use and scanning the network for the presence of IM software.

109. Remember that retention is critical.

The business community's failure to retain email and IM records is alarming. Check out these results from the *2006*

Workplace E-Mail, Instant Messaging & Blog Survey by the American Management Association and The ePolicy Institute:

Q: **Does your organization have a written policy governing email use and content?**

A: Yes   78.8%
    No   17.7%
    Unsure   3.5%

Q: **Does your organization have a written policy governing IM use and content?**

A: Yes   20.2%
    No   63.4%
    Unsure   16.4%

Q: **Do you know the difference between an electronic business record (email or IM) that must be retained, versus an insignificant message that may be deleted?**

A: Yes   63.1%
    No   23.6%
    Unsure   13.3%

110. Adhere to safety rules.

Thanks to better virus checkers, emails have become safer. However, IMs provide a new breeding ground for viruses and digital worms. Whether you're a veteran IM user or you just decided to take the plunge, here are some safety rules to remember:

On the technology side

- Run antivirus software regularly and apply security patches to your computer.

- Be sure your firewall is secure because IMs can dip into a firewall until they find an opening.

- Know that IMs can be saved and archived.

- Don't accept downloaded files from people you don't know.

On the common-sense side

- Never give out personal information such as your social security number, credit card numbers, passwords, and so forth.

- Never relay confidential or sensitive information.

- Monitor your children's use of IMs against a contact list or buddy list you've approved.

- Avoid posting your screen name online.

- Keep your business contacts on a list separate from family and friends.

- Follow company policies regarding the use of IMs.

 Some services let you archive IMs. If yours doesn't, you can cut and paste the message or the entire chat into a notepad or Word document.

Applying IM Etiquette

*A computer doesn't substitute for
good judgment any more than a pencil
substitutes for literacy.*

ROBERT S. MCNAMARA
The Essence of Security

Just as everyone is starting to get the hang of email etiquette (okay ... so not everyone), along comes another technology we need to think about. IMing can be a wonderful communications tool or it can be a tool with which people can embarrass themselves a hundred times faster than ever before.

111. Don't barge in.

Always introduce yourself, especially when starting an IM with a new contact. Before beginning a conversation, ask the recipient if she has a minute to chat with you. Being online doesn't mean the person at the other end is waiting for you. When you start a conversation, ask yourself the following: How would I approach the other person verbally? Where might be a good place to start the conversation? For example, you might begin, "Hi, is this a good time to discuss the Berger contract?" or "Hi, will you be at Bob's 2 PM mtg?"

Also, be respectful of coworkers. If they set their priority message to *busy*, perhaps it's a sign that they're working on a priority project and only want to be interrupted for urgent matters. Conversely, if you're on a priority project or tight deadline, set your default to *busy* so your colleagues will know you're not ignoring them.

 Don't send IMs to people at their offices unless you're sure it's okay.

112. Write carefully and thoughtfully.

Never write anything in an IM you wouldn't want posted on a billboard. Your message can be saved, forwarded, and used against you. This isn't the place to reprimand an employee, criticize a colleague, write IHMB (I hate my boss), or anything of that nature.

113. Think short.

Remember, the key word is *instant*, so be brief. If you are writing a lengthy response, let the recipient know beforehand so she doesn't think you're ignoring her while you're keying in the message. And send the message all at once, rather than a sentence or two at a time.

 If your conversation is going to be long-winded, pick up the phone.

114. **Be sensitive to other people's typing skills.**

You may be a whiz at keying in 100 words per minute, but not everyone else is. Be patient when waiting for a response from the hunt-and-peck set.

115. **Multitask realistically.**

Do you think you can talk on the phone and IM at the same time? Few people can multitask and remain on task. Besides taxing your communication skills, one or more of your messages will suffer. In the business world, this can be dangerous, especially with clients, customers, or vendors.

IMing lets you say hi to a friend or relative during the workday without being overheard on the phone. Chatting with acquaintances isn't what you're paid to do, so even though it may appear as if you're working, keep IMing in the office to a minimum.

116. **Avoid sloppy writing.**

Even though IMs are meant to be casual, never abandon good habits, especially in business situations.

- Don't use all caps.
- Don't use all lowercase.
- Use proper grammar and punctuation.

- Check for typos.

- Show your good manners by saying *THX* (thanks) and *PLS* or *PLZ* (please).

- End your message appropriately. Sign off with *TTYL* (talk to you later), *CFN* (ciao for now), *TAFN* (that's all for now), *EOM* (end of message), *CUL8R* (see you later), or something along those lines.

Remember that benign phrases such as *CUL8R* may be subject to interpretation. Do you mean "See you later today," "See you later this week," "See you later this year," or "See you later in this lifetime"? If you're using an ambiguous expression in a business context, you may need to be more specific.

117. Use abbreviations and emoticons.

DGOBWA (don't go overboard with abbreviations). Abbreviations are meant to keep messages concise yet meaningful. Use only those you're certain your reader will understand. (Check out Tip 122.) Use emoticons to convey your intentions, which can make up for the lack of gesticulations, facial expressions, and other body language. (Check out Tip 123.)

118. Be attuned to cultural differences.

You may be IMing with someone from another country or culture. Consider what you're saying and the impact it may have on the other person. If you're unsure of someone else's meaning, politely ask him to repeat it. (Check out Tip 6.)

119. Alert people when you're away.

IMing doesn't have a ring or busy signal as does the phone. When you're on an extended phone call or when you're away from your computer, consider leaving a default message that says, "Sorry, I'm not available right now" or "I'm away from the computer and will be back at noon."

120. Be considerate about inviting others into a session.

IMing is a wonderful way for team members to communicate in real time. Before you invite one or more people into a multiparty session, ask those already in the session for their approval.

121. Don't hide behind IMs.

IMs aren't intended to replace emails, face-to-face communication, or phone calls. Don't be an IM coward and use the technology to break up with your boyfriend or girlfriend, chastise a colleague, terminate an employee, or be confrontational.

Using Abbreviations and Showing Emotions

*A lot of fellows nowadays have a B.A.,
M.D., or Ph.D. Unfortunately they
don't have a J.O.B.*

FATS DOMINO
American singer

122. Pull letters out of the Scrabble box.

Although your friends may be IM-conversant, perhaps not all your business associates are. Use abbreviations sparingly or your message may look like a bowl of alphabet soup. Here are some common ones:

AAMOF	as a matter of fact
AFAIK	as far as I know
AFK	away from keyboard
AIM	AOL Instant Messenger
AM	away message
ASAP	as soon as possible
A/S/L	age/sex/location
ATM	at the moment

B	back
BBL	be back later
BBS	be back soon
BC	because
BCNU	be seein' you
BEG	big evil grin
BFN	bye for now
BFO	blinding flash of the obvious
BG	big grin
BI	buddy icon
BL	buddy list
BMG	be my guest
BRB	be right back
BTA	but then again
BTDT	been there, done that
BTW	by the way
CFN	ciao for now
CID	consider it done
CSG	chuckle snicker grin
CTRN	can't talk right now
CUL	see you later
CUL8R	see you later
CYL	catch you later
DHTB	don't have the bandwidth
DQMOT	don't quote me on this
EOM	end of message
FAQ	frequently asked questions
FTF	face to face
FWIW	for what it's worth
FYA	for your amusement
FYI	for your information

GAL	get a life
GL	good luck
GMTA	great minds think alike
GRA	go right ahead
GW	good work
HAND	have a nice day
H&K	hug and kiss
HT	hi there
HTH	hope this helps
IAC	in any case
IAE	in any event
IDK	I don't know
IHMB	I hate my boss
IK	I know
IKWUM	I know what you mean
I LV U	I love you / I'm leaving you [quite a difference]
IM	instant message
IMHO	in my humble opinion
IMNSHO	in my not so humble opinion
IMO	in my opinion
IMS	I'm sorry
IOW	in other words
JIC	just in case
JK	just kidding
JTLYK	just to let you know
K	okay
KIS	keep it simple
KWIM?	Know what I mean?
L8R	later

LOL	laughing out loud
MHBFU	my heart bleeds for you
MYOB	mind your own business
NBD	no big deal
NP	no problem
NRN	no response necessary
OBTW	oh, by the way
OH	offhand
OIC	oh, I see
OMG	oh my god / oh my gosh
OTL	out to lunch
OTOH	on the other hand
OTP	on the phone
PLS	please
PLZ	please
PMFJI	pardon me for jumping in
POC	point of contact
POS	parent over shoulder
POV	point of view
ROTFL	rolling on the floor laughing
RSN	real soon now
RUOK?	Are you okay?
SLAP	sounds like a plan
SN	screen name
SO	significant other
SYS	see you soon
TAFN	that's all for now
TBA	to be announced

TBH	to be honest
THX	thanks
TIA	thanks in advance
TTBOMK	to the best of my knowledge
TTFN	ta ta for now
TTYL	talk to you later
TY	thank you
UN	user name
WB	welcome back
WE	whatever
WFM	works for me
WRT	with respect to
WTG	way to go
WU?	What's up?
YCQMOT	you can quote me on this
YOYO	you're on your own
YT?	You there?
YW	you're welcome
YWSYLS	you win some, you lose some
ZOMG	oh my god / oh my gosh

A woman in one of my workshops who had just started IMing sent a message to her son. She wanted to appear IM-savvy and concluded the message with *LOL*, which she thought meant "lots of love." He and his friends were Laughing Out Loud over that.

123. **Use emoticons to show your emotions or intentions.**

Because IMs are short messages without much context, emoticons may help to convey your tone. These little symbols are especially useful when you want to clarify your true meaning, such as when you're saying something tongue-in-cheek. They're more appropriate for personal use than for business. Here are just a few common emoticons:

:-@	angry
:-S	confused
]:-)>	devilish
:-$	embarrassed
:-|	expressionless
:-)	happy
~&:-(	having a bad hair day
^5	high five
:-X	lips are sealed
8-)	rolling my eyes
:-(	sad
:-8	screaming
:-O	shouting

For an extensive listing of neat emoticons and graphics, check out **http://messenger.msn.com/Resource/ Emoticons.aspx**.

PART THREE

Text Messages,

Blogs,

and Chatrooms

When baby boomers entered the workforce, electronic messaging was in its infancy. Boomers relied on face-to-face contact as a way to build relationships. Now baby boomers are exiting the workforce and Generation Y'ers (also known as millennials, the millennial generation, and the net generation) are entering. Gen Y'ers are ravenous information gatherers, they're wired, they're more insular, and they see the world as a borderless marketplace. They engage in less face-to-face contact and don't limit themselves just to email and instant messaging. They podcast, they Google, they chat, they blog, they WiFi, they iPhone, they text message, they shop online, and they rely on hand-helds that do everything short of folding their laundry. Many Gen Y'ers regard email, fax, and voicemail as "last-millennium" technology used by Neanderthals such as their parents, teachers, and older coworkers.

As this demographic shift continues, faster and more accessible technology will continue to become more and more mainstream. It allows for flexible work schedules, making specific hours and dress codes archaic. Skilled workers are in more control of their locations. And collaborative work teams form and disband as projects and project requirements change.

With any of these technologies, however, identities can be obscure or ambiguous. People may lie about their identities, accounts may be compromised, and attackers may be listening to your conversations. You must always be vigilant and aware of the information you share—and that rings true for any technology.

Sending Text Messages

Get ready for the inbox on your phone to fill up faster. From fast-food chains to carmakers to consumer goods manufacturers and sports franchises, more and more companies are adopting text messaging as a way to target consumers on the move.... After all, more than 95 million Americans are considered active text messagers, according to the Yankee Group research firm. And marketers see it as low on cost and high in effectiveness.

DAVE CARPENTER
"Savvy Marketers Using Text Messaging,"
The Associated Press, September 24, 2006

Text messaging (commonly referred to as *texting*) is a quick, quiet, and easy way to send a person-to-person (P2P) message from your cell phone to someone else's cell phone, hand-held computer, pager, or email address. So when you're stuck in a meeting or you're at the library, you can stay in touch—silently. It's interesting to note that text-message marketing campaigns have already taken hold in Europe and Asia because corporations find it an easy and successful way to connect with consumers.

 Like any new technology, texting has its controversy and should be used with discretion. For example, it's creating quite a buzz in state legislatures where an increasing number of lawmakers text with staffers, family members, and lobbyists while sitting in chambers listening to debates. The National Conference of State Legislatures reports that more than half the states have passed regulations limiting the use of electronic devices during a legislative session. Critics charge that when the elected officials are texting, they're not paying attention to the session. The officials claim they use texting for constructive purposes, such as contacting staffers in order to research legislation or get instant feedback on speeches and controversial issues.

124. Understand the major advantages.

- Providers must be qualified and approved to use network carriers, so spams and scams are less likely than with other forms of communications technology.

- Cell phones play an important role in countries where the Internet is censored or not readily available.

- Messages can be downloaded so you respond when it's convenient.

- Messages can be saved in your phone's memory.

- You can text your teenager to remind him of the curfew.

125. Know the main drawbacks.

- Text messages are limited to a few hundred characters, so IMing or email may be more beneficial in some situations.

- You can't attach files.

- There's the potential for thumb injuries. (In Japan, people who text message are called *oyayubi-zoku*, or "thumb tribe." Just as computers may contribute to carpal tunnel syndrome, there are indications that texting may contribute to thumb-related ailments.)

- Texting can get out of control. In a study by Avaya Communications, 65 percent of those surveyed admitted to having texted someone who was in the same room, and 28 percent admitted to texting during a wedding or funeral.

126. Apply the rules of etiquette.

Dos

- Use texting for quick business messages. For example, you may write, "JTLYK will B late 4 sales mtg. L8R." (Translation: "Just to let you know, I'll be late for the sales meeting. See you later.")

- Think about the tone of your message. What may seem completely innocent to you may be misinterpreted by the recipient. This is where emoticons may be helpful. (Check out Tip 123.)

- Be attuned to people's schedules. Just because you're awake and working doesn't mean others are.

- Send love notes. Teens and twenty-somethings use texting to do just that. Recipients like it because they can save the messages and look at them whenever the urge strikes, whereas they won't carry written love notes around. But remember, unsaved messages disappear if your cell phone breaks or you lose it.

- Don't use texting to dump your girlfriend or boyfriend or end your marriage. ("I H8 U, loser!" is purported to be the message Britney Spears sent to Kevin Federline to end their marriage. A film crew from Canada's MuchMusic channel caught the shocked Federline on tape as he received the message on his BlackBerry.)

- Don't text while you're in the presence of other people. It's rude.

- Avoid texting while you're driving. It's bad enough to talk on the phone while you're driving, but pounding out a message is just plain dangerous.

- Don't text if you must get in touch with someone quickly. Pick up the phone.

127. Shut your phone off during meetings and in public places.

Unless your spouse, significant other, or partner is expecting to have a baby momentarily, turn your phone off during meetings. Whether you're speaking on the phone or texting, you're not engaged with the people in your group. Also turn it off in public places such as movie theaters, restaurants, concerts, museums, and so forth, where it can disturb other people.

I was having dinner at a posh restaurant. Sitting at the table next to me were three very well-dressed patrons each talking on cell phones during much of the dinner. When they weren't talking on their phones, they were texting and laughing at their messages. Perhaps they weren't enjoying each other's company. On another occasion, I was attending an opera at the Metropolitan Opera in New York, and someone's cell phone rang in the middle of the performance. The person answered in rather a loud voice, showing absolutely no regard for the performers or the audience.

 Include a section on text messages in your company policies. (Check out Tips 104–106, "Creating a Company Policy.")

Capitalizing on the Value of Blogs

Marketers say bloggers' unsolicited opinions and offhand comments are a source of invaluable insights that are hard to get elsewhere. "We look at the blogosphere as a focus group with 15 million people going on 24/7 that you can tap into without going behind a one-way mirror," says Rick Murray, executive vice president of Edelman, a Chicago public-relations firm.

WILLIAM M. BULKELEY
The Wall Street Journal Online,
January 15, 2004

Weblogs, commonly called blogs, appear to visitors as web pages with postings by one or more people in reverse chronological order. Blogs have come a long way since they were merely teenage ruminations on life (basically online diaries). With just a few clicks, every digital photo, PowerPoint presentation, email, government report, and more can be broadcast into the blogosphere. Blogging has grown into a completely new way of doing business. Bloggers share thoughts and ideas, foster personal relationships and communities, build personal and corporate credibility, and grab search-engine attention.

As an example of the impact blogging has made on the world stage, in 2007, *Time* magazine included the Chinese blogger and human rights activist Zeng Jinyan in their annual list of the world's 100 most influential people. Zeng started a blog when her husband was detained by the Chinese government without any legal proceedings.

 Include a section on blogs in your company policies. (Check out Tips 104–106, "Creating a Company Policy.")

128. Use a blog to facilitate team/project information sharing.

Blogs are very strong communications tools for teams and projects, and they are supplanting corporate intranets. As McDonald's CIO Dave Weick says, "Blogs are a way to bring our knowledge together." Blogs are being used at every level of savvy organizations because they . . .

- keep stakeholders in the loop.

- suggest an open-communication platform in the spirit of collaboration and learning.

- transfer information as a viable alternative to meetings.

- become a vehicle for sharing problems and garnering solutions.

- serve as a history of lessons learned.

 Unlike IMs or text messages, blogs are "time-shifted." A post often shows up instantly, but other bloggers often read the post sometime later. Most blogs offer the ability to "syndicate," which means interested users can subscribe to your blog and automatically be notified when you post new entries.

129. Use a blog to build your business.

A blog puts your name and your company out there, as does a website. You can post and update a blog yourself without the help of a web developer. Blogs are an easy way to communicate with customers, clients, and employees. And when you launch a public relations campaign, treat bloggers as if they're the press.

Here's a quick marketing tip: There's no need for emerging companies to go without a web presence while their websites are being developed. To get an instant web presence, check out some of the free blogs, such as

- www.blogger.com

- www.thefreesite.com/Free_Blog_Resources

- www.typepad.com

- www.myspace.com

- www.livejournal.com

- www.godaddy.com

Make your blog one people want to read. The more blogs that are linked to yours, the higher up you'll be in search engine rankings.

130. Decide if your blog will be a monologue or a dialogue.

Although some people and companies use monologue blogs as places to post articles, press releases, and more, there is great benefit in a dialogue. Realize, however, that this benefit comes with inherent risks. If you want to "talk" with your customers, expect to hear from those who are disgruntled, and be prepared to respond. Always remember that a customer who complains is one who wants to continue doing business with you and is giving you an opportunity to right a wrong. A customer who doesn't complain simply goes away (perhaps to your competitor).

Another reason for a dialogue is that people enjoy reading what others have posted, even though they may not post their own comments.

131. When dialoguing, remember that each blog is someone's web home.

Always be mindful that a blog is someone's Internet home, so be respectful and honest. If you aren't, you'll lose respect in the blogging community.

Dos

- When posting to a blog or contacting a blog host for the first time, introduce yourself. Include your name, location, URL, and blog (if you have one).

- Ask the blog host if she has time to chat.

- Get to the point.

- Provide something of value.

- You may be posting to a blog in another time zone or another country, so be sensitive to language and time differences.

- If you disagree with the blogger, tactfully say why and propose a solution or different point of view.

- Be courteous and use polite language.

- Post on topic and make sure your comments reflect the spirit of the blog.

- Allow breathing room for the blog host to respond.

- End by thanking the blog host for her time.

Taboos

- Don't get personal until you know someone well.

- Don't bash a product or service. If you're using the blog to offer comments, make the comments constructive.

- Don't be a spoiler and divulge information such as the ending to a hot new movie.

- Don't expect the blog host to respond immediately.

- Avoid too much jargon.

 For tips on how to build your business using blogs, check out
www.101publicrelations.com/bloggingforbusiness.html.

For tips on blogging safety for kids, check out
www.safekids.com.

Here are a few ways to maximize your blog's visibility through search engine optimization (SEO):

■ Treat each page in your blog as a separate entity.

■ Select key words or a key phrase appropriate for each page.

■ Repeat your key words or phrase throughout each page (without overdoing it).

■ Give each page a title that includes the key words or phrase.

 Stay tuned for the next generation of blogs—vlogs (video weblogs), which are increasing in popularity.

"Speaking" in Chatrooms

*If you don't have something nice to say,
don't say anything.*

ETHEL LORENZ
my mother, "the Wise"

Chatrooms are sites on a computer network where users can hold online conversations in real time with many people at once. A user types in a message and waits for someone else to type in a response. Messages may be directed at individuals or the group. Chatrooms are typically organized around specific themes, such as business, sports, politics, entertainment, or music, but they may also be on general topics. They are popular places to hang out, giving users a chance to meet new people anonymously, around the corner or around the world.

In business, chatrooms are like online conference calls. Through Campfire and other programs, you can invite clients, colleagues, or vendors to link to a chatroom on your intranet for internal communications. With travel costs skyrocketing, businesses are turning to video chats to communicate with distant clients, other branches, and other businesses. On the personal side, video chats let you look family and friends eye to eye through the magic of the Internet.

132. Use proper chatroom etiquette.

As chatrooms have become more sophisticated, many have guidelines and codes of ethics. If the chatroom has frequently asked questions (FAQs), check out the etiquette before you enter. Following are some general guidelines:

Dos

- Conduct yourself as if you were a guest in someone's home and there are children present. There may well be.

- Greet chatters who enter with a friendly "Hi" or "Welcome."

- When addressing comments or questions to a specific person, begin with that person's name—for example, "Jane, do you think ... ?"

- Recognize that this isn't the format to advertise or sell.

- Feel free to use a nickname because anonymity encourages free and open discussion.

- In a public chatroom, use the language that everyone else is using.

- Stay on topic or theme. If your chatroom is about politics, don't interject with thoughts about a great new sitcom.

- When you exit the room, say "Goodbye" or "Bye" until the last visitor leaves. (That's the same courtesy you'd give anyone in an actual room.)

Taboos

- Don't use vulgarities or obscenities.

- Never verbally abuse, attack, embarrass, or threaten a chatter.

- If you disagree with a chatter, don't be confrontational.

- Don't post personal information such as your email address, phone number, or anything that would compromise your location or identity. If you do, you are responsible for the outcome.

 Be aware that Homeland Security officials may monitor chatrooms.

133. Check your need for perfection at the door.

Although this may be a shock to the system at first, chatters don't always use proper grammar and punctuation. Chatting is a rapid-fire exchange of thoughts, ideas, and questions. Learn the abbreviations and emoticons. And most of all, let go and have fun. (Check out Tips 122 and 123.)

134. Educate your children on what is and isn't okay.

Chatrooms are popular with kids and teens, and predators know this. Therefore, chatting poses a particular threat for children of all ages. If you are a parent, always discuss chatroom safety with your children and always monitor their chats. Here are some safety tips:

- Explain to children the dangers of giving out personal information such as their real name, school, residence, email address, or phone number.

- Tell children never to send anyone photographs of themselves or anything that relates to them personally.

- Encourage children to select nicknames that don't disclose personal information, even their gender—for example, "Dapper Dash" is less revealing than "Detroit Dan."

135. Know your responsibility as a parent.

Here are several things to keep in mind:

- Consider keeping the computer in an open area where you can monitor activity.

- Know who's on your children's buddy lists.

- Advise your children to come to you with anything that makes them feel uncomfortable.

- Learn the chat lingo. (Check out Tips 122 and 123.)

- Set time boundaries so your children don't become addicted to chatting.

- Save copies of chatroom conversations in case you need to report a problem.

- If you see any hint of predatory activity, notify the police immediately.

 Include a section on chatrooms in your company policies. (Check out Tips 104–106, "Creating a Company Policy.")

INDEX

ABOUT THE AUTHOR

Sheryl Lindsell-Roberts was born and raised in the Big Apple. Although she's no longer *in* New York, she'll always be *of* New York.

Sheryl draws strength and inspiration from the world around her, from her friends, and from her family. She shares her life with Jon, her husband and best friend. She's been blessed with two awesome sons and three dear grandchildren, who are the center of her universe.

For more than twenty years she has been the Principal of Sheryl Lindsell-Roberts & Associates, a business writing and marketing communications firm that helps companies to be more profitable and productive through the written word. She also delivers business writing, technical writing, and email workshops that help participants to cut writing time by 30 to 50 percent and get the results they want.

Sheryl feels fortunate to have a job that would be her hobby if it wasn't her profession. Between writing and delivering workshops, she's written 20 books for the professional and humor markets. Some of her hot sellers are *135 Tips for Writing Successful Business Documents* and *Strategic Business Letters and E-mail*, both published by Houghton Mifflin; *Technical Writing for Dummies*, published by John Wiley; and *Loony Laws & Silly Statutes*, published by Sterling Publishing.

To learn more, please check out **www.sherylwrites.com**.